The Remaking
of the Medieval
World, 1204

REACTING TO THE PAST is an award-winning series of immersive role-playing games that actively engage students in their own learning. Students assume the roles of historical characters and practice critical thinking, primary source analysis, and argument, both written and spoken. Reacting games are flexible enough to be used across the curriculum, from first-year general education classes and discussion sections of lecture classes to capstone experiences, intersession courses, and honors programs.

Reacting to the Past was originally developed under the auspices of Barnard College and is sustained by the Reacting Consortium of colleges and universities. The Consortium hosts a regular series of conferences and events to support faculty and administrators.

Note to instructors: Before beginning the game you must download the Gamemaster's Materials, including an instructor's guide containing a detailed schedule of class sessions, role sheets for students, and handouts.

To download this essential resource, visit https://reactingconsortium.org/games, click on the page for this title, then click "Instructors Guide."

The Remaking of the Medieval World, 1204

THE FOURTH CRUSADE

JOHN J. GIEBFRIED AND
KYLE C. LINCOLN

BARNARD

The University of North Carolina Press

Chapel Hill

The University of North Carolina Press has been a member of the
Green Press Initiative since 2003.

Cover illustration: Detail from Bodleian Library, MS 587, fol. 1r.

ISBN 978-1-4696-6411-8 (pbk.: alk. paper)
ISBN 978-1-4696-6412-5 (e-book)

The Fourth Crusade is in chaos. Its leaders had hoped that by diverting to Constantinople they would pay off their debts, secure Byzantine aid, and win the obedience of the Greek Orthodox Church for the papacy. Now the emperor they installed has been brutally murdered, and his killer sits on the Byzantine throne. The Crusaders must now decide: Should they let this crime go unpunished and continue on to Jerusalem, or should they dare to attack the largest, richest, and most well-defended city in the Christian world? Students will play as Crusaders from one of four historical factions—the Northern French, Imperial, Venetian, or Clerical Crusaders—each with unique personal and faction goals. In the end they will reenact the moment that changed Crusading and the relationship between the Eastern and Western Christian worlds forever.

Contents

PART FIVE: PRIMARY SOURCES

Part One

GAME OVERVIEW

Prologue
Murder in Constantinople

Forgive me, Father, for I have sinned. It has been, well, let's see, more than a year since my confession on the lagoon in Venice. When we heard the call to crusade preached by the Cistercian brothers of the abbey of Bonmont near the shores of Lac Leman, our father had the highest of hopes for the Holy Land, but we didn't know anything about the venture. It was a hard trip back for him across the Jura Mountains to our farm in Cologny, with cross sown on his travelling cloak, where our little farm makes the finest cheeses for the lords of Gex near Geneva. By the time he came home, he was already taken with consumption.

He passed away that November and my brother, William and I held together our farm through the snows. When spring came, the parish priest told us the bishop of Geneva had decreed we could send money to support a soldier fighting for the marquis in the crusade, or one of us could go in Father's stead. I made my way toward Venice with my father's cross sown on my shoulder and a sword on my back, carrying with me the staff of a humble and penitent pilgrim.

You know the rest, Father. We all grew hungry on the lagoon, waiting for the armies to arrive. When the day finally came to set out for Jerusalem, there were celebrations, and the wind was swift those first nights. It was my first time on a boat like that—not a little river skiff or a ferry, I mean. In those days, it was exciting, if a little hard on the belly. Now, I don't think I will ever stomach another long boat ride without getting sick for what has happened.

When we made landfall outside that city, I asked one of the Venetian sailors what the name of the town was called and how long we were staying. I can't remember his answer to the second question, but I remember the first one. Oh, God forgive us, I will hear the name of that city with my last breath: Zara. Word came down from the doge and the counts that the town was supposed to be in the hands of a good Christian who would give us aid and supplies and that maybe even more soldiers would join us.

3

There was a troubadour from Provence named Raimbaut, whom I had befriended on our passage. His dialect was thick, but eventually we understood each other. We talked to pass the time, mostly with the others on our round-ship, and it was a pleasant trip, mostly. The sun and the spray of the ships made my face feel fine. When we got to Zara we were tired, and Raimbaut looked more pale and yellow than he should have on our second day at Zara. He told me that the king whose town Zara was had betrayed God and the church and we had received orders to capture the town and take what supplies we could to avenge the dishonors done to Christ Jesus. Many lords, abbots, and knights left our company there, sailing on without aid of supplies to Jerusalem. Many nights I wish I had been brave enough to join them. Instead, I helped load a trebuchet that tossed stone after stone against the city's walls, killing many brave Christian men who defended the battlements.

By the time we made it to Constantinople, the count of Biandrate, told us in the *Gray Stork*, which was our round-ship, that we were sailing first to deliver the emperor of Constantinople to his palace. He had been betrayed by a dastardly uncle who deposed and barbarically blinded the boy's father and true emperor. The palaces and the churches of the Queen of Cities were being held hostage by the usurper, and the count said that we, by order of the Lord Pope Innocent, were to go honorably to his aid so that he would be restored to the place that God himself had destined him to hold.

I never saw the emperor when we were travelling, and I think I saw him only once while we were assembled on the plain outside the city. I know that he was young, or at least that he was called Alexius the Young. Raimbaut said that this was common on pilgrimages like ours. The emperors of Constantinople often pretended to love God and honor the church, but instead they double-crossed many. Even the great German emperors Conrad III and Frederick Barbarossa had been betrayed by the emperors of Constantinople when they had come in the time of our fathers and grandfathers. Raimbaut's friend Pierre told me that we were probably going to have to fight to defend the true emperor of Constantinople, since he was a pilgrim like we were. Pilgrims were bound by honor and their vows to defend one another. Even if the emperor of Constantinople did not obey the pope, he was a brother Christian too. This emperor, the young one, had promised to bring the church back together. Conduct that honorable was proof enough of his noble heart and his faithfulness. Or so we thought, Father.

That was some time ago. Since then, the young emperor has been deposed and murdered by a monster—who like every other Greek seems to be named Alexius. The traitor-emperor has attacked our ships and proven himself not only dishonorable but also a heathen, damned with the devil. So here we sit, waiting for the marquis, the doge, and the other lords to decide how best to attack those walls.

Those walls are taller than the tallest tree on our farm, Father, taller than the cathedral in Geneva. I've never seen any like them. I don't know how we'll get past them. I think that unless God has more mercy for my family yet, I will not survive an attack on those walls. I know that I have sinned many times on this journey, but if I don't make it to Jerusalem to fulfill my vow, I have done everything to remain true to my vow to take up the cross. Father, forgive me for what I must do in the name of the true church and in the name of the pilgrimage and with the blessings of the work of Christ. In the name of the Father, and of the Son, and of the Holy Ghost. Amen.

How to Play This Game

This is a "reacting" game. Reacting games are interactive historical role-playing games. Students are given elaborate game books, which place them in moments of historical controversy and intellectual ferment. The class becomes a public body of some sort; students, in role, become particular persons from the period, often as members of a faction. Their purpose is to advance a policy agenda and achieve their victory objectives. To do so, they will undertake research and write speeches and position papers; and they will also give formal speeches, participate in informal debates and negotiations, and otherwise work to win the game. After a few preparatory lectures, the game begins and the players are in charge; the instructor serves as adviser or "game master." Outcomes sometimes differ from the actual history; a postmortem session at the end of the game sets the record straight.

The following is an outline of what you will encounter in reacting games and what you will be expected to do. While these elements are typical of every reacting game, it is important to remember that every game has its own special quirks.

1. GAME SETUP

Your instructor will spend some time before the beginning of the game helping you to understand the historical background. During the set-up period, you will read several different kinds of material:

> the game book (which you are reading now), which includes historical information, rules and elements of the game, and essential documents
> your role, which describes the historical person you will play in the game

You may also be required to read primary and secondary sources outside the game book (perhaps including one or more accompanying books) to provide additional information and arguments for use during the game. Often you will be expected to conduct research to bolster your papers and speeches.

Read all of this contextual material and all of these documents and sources before the game begins. And just as important, go back and reread these materials throughout the game. A second reading while in role will deepen your understanding and alter your perspective; ideas take on a different aspect when seen through the eyes of a partisan actor.

Players who have carefully read the materials and who know the rules of the game will invariably do better than those who rely on general impressions and uncertain recollections.

2. GAME PLAY

Once the game begins, certain players preside over the class sessions. These presiding officers may be elected or appointed. Your instructor then becomes the game master (GM) and takes a seat in the back of the room. While not in control, the GM may do any of the following:

- pass notes to spur players to action;
- announce the effects of actions taken inside the game on outside parties (e.g., neighboring countries) or the effects of outside events on game actions (e.g., a declaration of war); and
- interrupt and redirect proceedings that have gone off track. (Presiding officers may act in a partisan fashion, speaking in support of particular interests, but they must observe basic standards of fairness.)

As a failsafe device, most reacting games employ the "Podium Rule," which allows a player who has not been recognized to approach the podium and wait for a chance to speak. Once at the podium, the player has the floor and must be heard. In order to achieve the character's objectives, outlined in your role sheet, you must persuade others to support your position. You must speak with others, because never will a role contain all that you need to know,

and never will one faction have the strength to prevail without allies. Collaboration and coalition-building are at the heart of every game.

Most role descriptions contain secret information that you are expected to guard. Exercise caution when discussing your role with others. You may be a member of a faction, which gives you allies who are generally safe and reliable, but even they may not always be in total agreement with you. In games where factions are tight-knit groups with fixed objectives, finding a persuadable ally can be difficult.

Fortunately, every game includes roles that are undecided (or "indeterminate") about certain issues. Everyone is predisposed on certain issues, but most players can be persuaded to support particular positions. Cultivating these players is in your interest. (By contrast, if you are assigned an indeterminate role, you will likely have considerable freedom to choose one or another side in the game; but often, too, indeterminates have special interests of their own.)

Cultivate friends and supporters. Before you speak at the podium, arrange to have at least one supporter second your proposal, come to your defense, or admonish those in the body not paying attention. Feel free to ask the presiding officer to assist you, but appeal to the GM only as a last resort. Immerse yourself in the game. Regard it as a way to escape imaginatively from your usual "self" and your customary perspective as a college student in the twenty-first century.

At first, this may cause discomfort because you may be advocating ideas that are incompatible with your own beliefs. You may also need to take actions that you would find reprehensible in real life. Remember that a reacting game is only a game and that you and the other players are merely playing roles. When they offer criticisms, they are not criticizing you as a person. Similarly, you must never criticize another person in the game. But you will likely be obliged to criticize their persona. (For example, never say, "Sally's argument is ridiculous."

But feel free to say, Doge Dandolo's argument is ridiculous"—though you would do well to explain exactly why!) Always assume, when spoken to by a fellow player—whether in class or out of class—that that person is speaking to you in role.

Help to create this world by avoiding the colloquialisms and familiarities of today's college life. For example, never should the presiding officer open a session with the salutation "Hi, guys." Similarly, remember that it is inappropriate to trade on out-of-class relationships when asking for support within the game. ("Hey, you can't vote against me. We're both on the tennis team!")

Reacting games seek to approximate of the complexity of the past. Because some people in history were not who they seemed to be, so too some roles in reacting games may include elements of conspiracy or deceit. (For example, Brutus did not announce to the Roman Senate his plans to assassinate Caesar.) If you are assigned such a role, you must make it clear to everyone that you are merely playing a role. If, however, you find yourself in a situation where you find your role and actions to be stressful or uncomfortable, tell the GM.

3. GAME REQUIREMENTS

Your instructor will explain the specific requirements for your class. In general, a reacting game will require you to perform several distinct but interrelated activities:

- **Reading.** This standard academic work is carried on more purposefully in a reacting course, since what you read is put to immediate use.
- **Research and writing.** The exact writing requirements depend on your instructor, but in most cases you will be writing to persuade others. Most of your writing will take the form of policy statements, but you might also write autobiographies, clandestine messages,

newspapers, or after-game reflections. In most cases papers are posted on the class website for examination by others. Basic rules: Do not use big fonts or large margins. Do not simply repeat your position as outlined in your role sheets. You must base your arguments on historical facts as well as ideas drawn from assigned texts—and from independent research. (Your instructor will outline the requirements for footnoting and attribution.) Be sure to consider the weaknesses in your argument and address them; if you do not, your opponents will.

- **Public speaking and debate.** Most players are expected to deliver at least one formal speech from the podium (the length of the game and the size of the class will affect the number of speeches). Reading papers aloud is seldom effective. Some instructors may insist that students instead speak freely from notes. After a speech, a lively and even raucous debate will likely ensue. Often the debates will culminate in a vote.
- **Strategizing.** Communication among students is a pervasive feature of reacting games. You should find yourself writing emails, texting, and attending meetings on a fairly regular basis. If you do not, you are being outmaneuvered by your opponents.

4. SKILL DEVELOPMENT

A recent Associated Press article on education and employment made the following observations:

The world's top employers are pickier than ever. And they want to see more than high marks and the right degree. They want graduates with so-called soft skills—those who can work well in teams, write and speak with clarity, adapt quickly to changes in technology and business conditions, and interact with colleagues from different countries and cultures. . . . And companies are going to ever-greater lengths to identify the students who have the right mix of skills, by observing them in role-playing exercises to see how they handle pressure and get along with others . . . and [by] organizing contests that reveal how students solve problems and handle deadline pressure.[1]

Reacting, probably better than most elements of the curriculum, provides the opportunity for developing these "soft skills." This is because you will be practicing persuasive writing, public speaking, critical thinking, problem-solving, and collaboration. You will also need to adapt to changing circumstances and to work under pressure.

1. Paul Wiseman, "Firms Seek Grads who Can Think Fast, Work in Teams," Associated Press, July 1, 2013.

Counterfactuals

This game strives for historical accuracy as much as possible, but a few liberties have been taken to create a more robust debate. Although all the characters in the game are historical figures active in Constantinople in the time of the Fourth Crusade, not all of them would have been able to be part of the deliberations this game recreates. All the indeterminates and some of the lower-ranking Venetians fall into this category. More importantly, the characters of Empress Anna and Theodore Branas—although sympathetic to the Crusaders—were inside Constantinople in March 1204, but this game has taken liberties to say they snuck out to join the deliberations. Likewise, the character of King Lalibela requires some explanation. Robert of Clari mentions that the "king of Nubia" was in Constantinople in later 1203. This game accepts Benjamin Hendrickx's suggestion that this king was, in fact, King (or Negus) Gebre Mesqel Lalibela of Ethiopia. There is no evidence of what he did during the Fourth Crusade—perhaps he had even left before the attack on Constantinople—but this game posits that he remained at the Crusader camp, at least until the deliberations began.

Part Two

HISTORICAL BACKGROUND

Timeline of the Fourth Crusade

1195

Byzantine Emperor Alexius III deposes and blinds his brother, Emperor Isaac II

1198

January 8th: Innocent III is elected pope

August: Pope Innocent III calls the Fourth Crusade

1199

November 28th: Thibaut of Champagne, Louis of Blois, and others join the Fourth Crusade at the Tournament at Écry

1200

February 23rd: Baldwin of Flanders takes the cross and joins the Fourth Crusade

1201

Late Winter/ Early Spring: Isaac II's son, Prince Alexius, escapes from his uncle, Alexius III, and comes to the West

April: Crusader envoys travel to Venice and make a contract with Enrico Dandolo

May 24th: Death of Thibaut of Champagne, initial leader of the Fourth Crusade

August: Boniface of Montferrat becomes the leader of the Fourth Crusade

1202

Summer: Many Crusaders arrive in Venice, although far less than anticipated

October: The Crusader army departs Venice

November: The Crusader army besieges the Christian city of Zara

December: Emissaries of Prince Alexius arrive at Zara to discuss an alliance

1203

May: Prince Alexius arrives at the Crusader camp

June 23rd: The Crusade arrives at Constantinople

July 17th: Crusaders attack Constantinople

July 18th: Emperor Alexius III flees, Isaac II is reinstated by the Greeks

August 1st: Prince Alexius is crowned alongside his father as Co-Emperor Alexius IV

December: Tensions escalate over Alexius IV's unpaid debts to the Crusaders

1204

January 27th: Alexius Ducas "Murtzuphlus" leads a coup and imprisons Alexius IV

February 8th: Alexius IV is murdered on the orders of Murtzuphlus

March: Our game begins

From Constantine to the Crusades

The Road to 1204

In hoc signo vinces—In this sign you will conquer. Such was the message written in the clouds that a Roman general saw on the morning of October 28, 312, as he prepared to meet his rival outside Rome at the Battle of the Milvian Bridge. Ancient historians cannot agree if that heavenly sign was a cross or the Greek letters *chi* and *rho*— but they agree that the general who painted this image on the shields of his men promptly won the battle and marched into Rome and the history books as the **Emperor Constantine**.

Thus begins the story of Rome's first Christian emperor. While Constantine did not make Christianity the official religion of the Roman Empire, he shifted the balance of power between Christianity and Greco-Roman polytheism. No longer would Christians be persecuted by the Roman state; instead Rome would help shape and spread Christianity across the world. Under his leadership, the first **ecumenical council** of all the bishops of the church would meet at **Nicaea** and create a set of orthodox doctrines for the Christian world and a unified creed. This council would be one of his lasting achievements, not only because that Nicene Creed is still recited today, but also because his council set a precedent whereby in proceeding centuries, generations of bishops and abbots, often under the patronage of an emperor, would meet at similar councils to reach consensus on other issues of faith.

Constantine's other lasting legacy was the city he built—**Constantinople**. This was to be a new capital for his empire—a New Rome—built by dragging pieces of the old Rome to his new city built on the border of Europe and Asia, controlling the passage between the Black Sea and the Mediterranean. It would become a global trade center and one of the most strategic chokepoints in world history. At his death, his heirs divided the empire between themselves: a Western Roman Empire based in Rome and an Eastern Roman Empire ruled from Constantinople.

In the years after Constantine's death, increasing tensions between the Romans and the

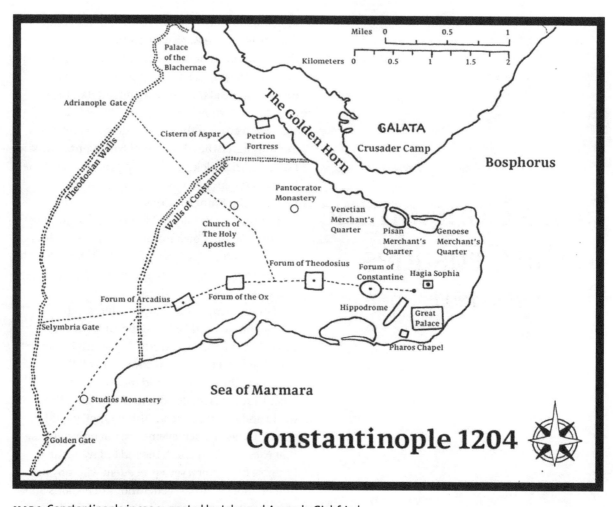

The following labels appear on the map:

Palace of the Blachernae
Adrianople Gate
Cistern of Aspar
Petrion Fortress
Theodosian Walls
Walls of Constantine
The Golden Horn
GALATA
Crusader Camp
Bosphorus
Pantocrator Monastery
Venetian Merchant's Quarter
Pisan Merchant's Quarter
Genoese Merchant's Quarter
Church of The Holy Apostles
Forum of Theodosius
Forum of Constantine
Hagia Sophia
Forum of Arcadius
Forum of the Ox
Hippodrome
Great Palace
Selymbria Gate
Pharos Chapel
Studios Monastery
Sea of Marmara
Golden Gate
Constantinople 1204

Miles 0   0.5   1
Kilometers 0   0.5   1   1.5   2

MAP 1 Constantinople in 1204, created by John and Amanda Giebfried.

Germanic peoples living along their frontiers led to a succession of wars and invasions. While the emperor of the Eastern Empire was killed in battle with the Germanic Goths in 378, it was the Western Empire that suffered the brunt of these "barbarian invasions." Rome was sacked three times in the 400s, and its last emperor was deposed in 476 by a Germanic warlord. The East endured, in large part due to the strategic and highly defensible position of Constantinople, surrounded on three sides by the sea and on the fourth side by a set of formidable double walls built in the early 400s. These **Theodosian Walls**, named for the emperor who built them, would hold off a millennium of would-

be conquerors, starting with the infamous Attila the Hun and lasting until the Ottoman Empire blasted through them with gigantic gunpowder cannons in 1453.

Despite no longer ruling from the city of Rome, emperors in Constantinople would continue calling themselves Romans for another millennium. Over time, Greek would replace Latin as the language of the Eastern Roman court, and so later Renaissance historians would dub these rulers "Byzantine"—a reference to the small Greek village of Byzantium, on top of which Constantine built his imperial capital. This empire would face centuries of threats from the East, first from the

Persians and later from the Muslim Arabs. The latter conquest would strip away Byzantine possessions in Egypt, North Africa, Palestine and Syria—but the core lands of Anatolia and the Balkans would remain in their possession.

In the West, the task of carrying on the legacy of Constantine fell not to an emperor but instead to the church. The symbolic moment of transition came when, as Attila the Hun ravaged his way across Northern Italy, it was Rome's bishop, and not the emperor, who rode out to meet the conqueror and convinced him to turn back. The bishop of Rome, later known as the pope, was the heir to St. Peter and was considered by the earliest church councils to be the "first among equals" among the bishops of the Christian world—just as Peter had been among the original disciples.

Now the pope was by no means the all-powerful voice in the Christian church. In fact, tradition held there to be five **patriarchs**—located in Rome, Constantinople, Antioch, Alexandria, and Jerusalem—who shared the governance of the church and oversaw the bishops in their regions. This group was known as the **Pentarchy**. The Arab conquests displaced the latter three patriarchs, leaving Rome and Constantinople as the only two with any effective authority. However, both these patriarchs had to contend with the emperors in Constantinople. These temporal rulers believed that they had an oversight role within the church, which included calling and presiding over church councils, promulgating edicts to regulate the church and clergy, nominating a candidate to become a pope or patriarch, and as necessary removing a pope or patriarch of Constantinople who opposed them. This was the doctrine of **caesaropapism**, and while by about the year 750 Rome asserted its ecclesiastical independence from the emperor, the patriarch of Constantinople remained under the emperor's thumb for the whole of the empire's history.

In Western Europe, political power shifted from an emperor in Rome to a set of Germanic kings who divided up the old Roman world. However, running parallel to that secular state was an ecclesiastical hierarchy that retained many of its Roman features. The bishops of the era came from former elite Roman families, the dioceses they presided over took their names and shapes from the provinces (called dioceses) of the late Roman Empire, the language of the church remained Latin, and the bishops acknowledged the pope in Rome as their spiritual head. The church worked to convert the Germanic kings of the West, both those who were followers of the Old Germanic gods and those who practiced forms of Christianity deemed heretical by the early church councils. Once in the fold, the church worked alongside these kings to administer their new states. As their authority grew, the church became more involved in politics. So when an ambitious Frankish nobleman whose family had ruled the kingdom in all but name for two generations wanted to justify overthrowing the ruling dynasty, he went to the pope in Rome for approval.

Medieval Europe was fundamentally transformed by that new king's son, who went down in history as Charles the Great, or **Charlemagne**. He expanded his empire, becoming master of much of modern Western Europe

Charlemagne also led a cultural renaissance, working hand in hand with the church to preserve and distribute old Latin texts, promote education, and reform church and civil society. Although he controlled an empire larger than that of the emperors in Constantinople, Charlemagne was known only as the king of the Franks. This changed on Christmas Day in the year 800, when the pope crowned him emperor in Rome. It is hard to say whether the pope meant this as a return to an era of two emperors, as had existed in the late Roman world, or whether he meant for Charlemagne to be the one true emperor (a claim made easier by the fact that the ruler in Constantinople at the time was an empress who had killed her son in her rise to power). Nevertheless, for the rest of the medieval era there would now be two emperors, one in the East and the other in the West.

Charlemagne's unified empire was later divided among his grandsons. These three kingdoms of East, Middle, and West Francia fought among each other over the next several generations, leading to a fracturing of political and ethnic identities. The kingdom of the West Franks evolved into France, and the kingdom of the East Franks became Germany—and after a new dynasty consolidated both East and Middle Francia, and like Charlemagne received a papal coronation—a German-dominated **Holy Roman Empire** emerged.

The disintegration of Charlemagne's empire coincided with a series of external invasions—most importantly the nomadic Magyars attacking from the East and the Vikings from the North. This not only caused an increase in fortifications, leading toward the stone castles that are emblematic of the medieval West, but also to a political and economic transformation. Frankish kings needed to field large armies to fight their wars but did not have the centralized bureaucracy to support them on their own. Instead, they granted land to mounted warriors if they agreed to fight for their lord in times of war. What emerged was a system commonly called **feudalism**. There was no one perfect model of how feudalism worked, and regional variations were numerous, but in its simplest form feudalism was a set of reciprocal obligations between the military elite. In the transaction, one man was the lord—the owner of a piece of land, traditionally called a **fief**—and the other was the **vassal**, who would rule over that fief in return for a specified set of obligations, normally including military service to his lord. When the vassal died, his heirs would inherit the fief if they agreed to continue their obligations to the lord's family. Feudalism is often depicted as a pyramid, with the king on top, lords in the middle, knights below them, and peasants working the land at the bottom. This is a radical oversimplification, since all members of the warrior-aristocracy from kings to common knights could own multiple fiefs from different lords, some of equal or lower rank to themselves. Even kings could be vassals—English

kings held fiefs in France, for which they were vassals to the king of France, but for their lands in England they answered to no lord. Counts of **Flanders** held fiefs from both the king of France and the Holy Roman Empire and thus could not be considered direct vassals of either; moreover, they granted out part of their land as a fief to the Count of **Saint-Pol**, who despite being of equal rank, still was a vassal of the Count of Flanders.

As a result, historians have extended the feudal system to include more than just the military aristocracy. They speak instead of a feudal society, where the peasants who worked the land were likewise tied to the owners of the fiefs by a series of reciprocal obligations—normally the protection and justice of the lord, in return for payment in cash or more commonly in a portion of the agricultural surplus. This relationship, however, varies to an even greater degree than the one within the military aristocracy, making any generalization of it all but impossible.

Just as the disintegration of Charlemagne's empire had led to a restructuring of the political system, so too was it responsible for a reformation of the Catholic Church. Without the hand of an emperor, either Western or Eastern, to watch over them, the leading families of Rome turned the papacy into a political tool in their many rivalries. The men and teenage boys elected pope in this period were too busy killing their rivals, sleeping with their mistresses, and putting the corpses of their predecessors on trial to effectively govern the spiritual affairs of the world. Thus, the great papal reform movement began not in Rome but in the monasteries of France and Germany, and they were carried to Rome by the German Holy Roman Emperors, who like their Greek predecessors began to effectively appoint popes from the mid-tenth century until the mid-eleventh century. During this period of reform, the church banned the sale of church offices, imposed clerical celibacy, appointed senior clerics as cardinals who would help administer the church and elect the next pope, and attempted to ban the practice of lay investiture—that is, having a secular lord appoint the bishops within his land. This last reform was unacceptable to the Holy Roman Emperors, and during the mid-eleventh century a power struggle ensued between the pope and the emperor—which ended with a compromise giving the emperor some input in the selection of bishops. At the heart of this conflict between church and state was one of the central philosophical arguments of the medieval West—**the doctrine of the two swords**. This was first formulated by an early medieval pope who argued that there were two sources of power in the world, which later authors explained with the gospel metaphor of the two swords—one spiritual and one secular. Of these two swords, the spiritual sword was held to be predominant—a fact contested throughout the Middle Ages by kings and emperors wielding their secular swords.

During the era of papal reform, the patriarchates of Rome and Constantinople moved further and further apart on issues of religious importance. For centuries there had been disputes about the respective authority of the pope in Rome and the patriarch in Constantinople. Each side could point to conflicting early church councils that accepted both the primacy of Rome and the coequality of the five patriarchs. However, the rift was more than just about politics: the doctrines and practices of the churches subject to Rome and Constantinople had been growing increasingly out of sync over the centuries. Some of this was purely cultural: Latin was the language of the church in Western Europe, and Greek was the language in the East. Greek priests could marry and used leavened bread (containing yeast) in their celebrations of the Eucharist; Latin priests were theoretically celibate and used unleavened (excluding yeast) bread. Moreover, to deal with a theological controversy in Spain, clerics in Rome amended the text of the creed established at the Council of Nicaea to say that the Holy Spirit proceeded not just from God the Father but also from Jesus the Son. This was done to head off an argument that the Son was not equal to the Father,

and the addition to the creed became known as the *filioque* **clause** because *filioque* means "and the son" in Latin. While this change was widely accepted across the West, it was a major point of contention with the Greeks, who saw it as a major theological redefinition of God, which could only be endorsed by a new church council. Tensions boiled over in the mid-800s when the imperially appointed patriarch of Constantinople, named Photius, ratcheted up tensions by accusing the Western church of heresy, specifically over the issues of papal supremacy and the *filioque* clause. Once the emperor removed Photius, the issue died down for two centuries. However, in 1054 a cardinal sent from Rome to Constantinople on a diplomatic mission reopened the dispute and excommunicated the patriarch of Constantinople; in return, the patriarch excommunicated the cardinal. While this was a personal excommunication, not two churches excommunicating all the faithful of the other church, the moment marked a major rift between East and West. For the next several centuries there were attempts to reunite the churches, but these major theological and doctrinal issues continued to divide a once united church.

In the East, the emperors in Constantinople had been largely successful in driving back their Arab and Bulgarian rivals and were having a new golden age in the early eleventh century. That all changed, however, with the emergence of the Seljuq Turks. Between the death of the Prophet Mohammed and the late ninth century, the Islamic world was led by a series of caliphs—literally the successors to the Prophet Mohammed—who ruled as the spiritual and temporal heads of the Sunni Islamic world. They had attempted to fight their way through Constantinople's Theodosian Walls several times, all without success. The height of medieval Islamic civilization came under the Sunni **Abbasid dynasty**, which established the city of Baghdad as its capital. However, the Abbasids faced a threat from a pair of rival Shia dynasties. The first, known as the **Fatimids**, who set themselves up in North

Africa and Egypt and expanded into neighboring Palestine. In 1009, a Fatimid caliph mercilessly persecuted Christians, something prohibited under Islamic law, and destroyed Jerusalem's Church of the Holy Sepulcher, the holiest site in the Christian world. This event, nearly a century later, would be part of the impetus for the First Crusade. The second rival dynasty, known as the Buyids, managed to capture Persia and later seize Baghdad itself. The Abbasids turned to a Turkish warlord from Central Asia who drove the Buyids from Baghdad and then established himself as the sultan of the Seljuq Sultanate. He took over day-to-day rulership of Mesopotamia, Persia, and Eastern Anatolia, leaving the caliph as a largely ceremonial figure. Although the sultan married the daughter of the caliph, he died childless, and Turkish power fragmented between his many relatives. His nephew invaded Anatolia in 1071 and decisively defeated the Byzantine emperor at the battle of **Manzikert**. For the first time, a sitting emperor was captured in battle. Byzantium had to surrender much of Eastern Anatolia, including the strategic city of Antioch. However, this defeat was just the beginning, and a decade-long civil war broke out among the Byzantines. During the chaos, the Turks expanded westward, taking almost all of Anatolia from the Greeks. The victor in the civil war was a general named **Alexius Comnenus**, who shortly after coming to the throne called upon the pope in Rome, asking for western military aid against the Turks.

The call was picked up by **Pope Urban II**, who called the **First Crusade** on November 27, 1095. Speaking at a local church council in Clermont, France, he lamented the advance of the Turks and the destruction of the Church of the Holy Sepulcher, and so he asked for volunteers to go east to aid their eastern Christian kinsmen and liberate Jerusalem in return for the remission of all their sins. The message and movement quickly blossomed in the hands of travelling preachers. Soon, instead of the small elite force of a few thousand knights that the Byzantine emperor had envi-

sioned, the pope was trying to wrangle a popular movement of 30,000 to 50,000 people. He appointed a French bishop to be his representative on the expedition, but before the main army could travel east, an unruly and unprepared contingent known as the Peoples' Crusade made its way across Europe. This undisciplined rabble shocked Alexius I by pillaging Greek Christian towns for supplies on their way to Constantinople. Alexius transported them across the Bosporus, where they were swiftly annihilated by the Turkish army.

The main contingent would not suffer the same fate. It was led by some of the preeminent lords of the medieval West, including the counts of Toulouse, Flanders, and Blois, and Duke Godfrey of Bouillon. It arrived in Constantinople over the winter of 1096–97, and like the Peoples' Crusade, it skirmished with the Greeks over access to the promised food and supplies. Additionally, before these Crusaders were allowed to continue, Emperor Alexius insisted that they swear an oath to return any conquered land to him, as its rightful ruler. The army retook Nicaea with Greek aid and defeated the Turks before being worn down in a long siege of Antioch. During the siege a small force of Crusaders seized power in the Armenian Christian city of Edessa, securing its help for the Crusader army. After a year outside the gates of Antioch and with word of a Turkish army on its way, the Crusaders sent the Count of Blois as an envoy to ask again for Greek help. When it wasn't forthcoming, he fled home rather than returning to the Crusader host, which brought him only shame, especially in the eyes of his wife, a daughter of the English king William the Conqueror. The situation looked bleak, but then an Armenian turncoat opened the city's gates to the Crusaders. Once inside, the army found a relic purporting to be the Holy Lance, which pierced Christ's side on the cross. With it the army rode out into battle, defeating a much larger Turkish force. Since Alexius had not come to their aid, many Crusaders felt their oaths to him were no longer binding, and so they kept Antioch and the rest of their conquests in the

Holy Land for themselves. In 1099 the Crusaders marched further south and finally took Jerusalem, massacring thousands of Muslim residents as they did so. The question now became over who should rule the city, and the leading warlords' squabbles over the crown almost scuttled the entire Crusade. Eventually leaders settled the disagreement by granting Jerusalem to Duke Godfrey and the lesser lordships to other leading barons.

For the next seven decades, the heirs of these Crusaders would rule a quartet of Crusader states: the kingdom of Jerusalem, the principality of Antioch, and the counties of Tripoli and Edessa There they opened the ways for Christian pilgrims to visit their holiest sites in peace and intermarried with and worked alongside the Eastern Christians of the Holy Land, especially the Armenians. However, as the century progressed, they faced increasingly dangerous Muslim enemies. In 1144, the County of Edessa was conquered by the Turkish emir of Mosul, precipitating the Second Crusade.

When the First Crusade ended with the successful capture of Jerusalem, there was no expectation that this would be more than just a one-time event. It had been a great triumph for those who participated, but a generation later a Second Crusade to retake Edessa gave a new generation the chance to follow in their fathers' footsteps. In the following century, the definition of what was or was not a Crusade was gradually hammered out. Although there is no accepted medieval definition, scholars today generally argue that a Crusade was a military expedition called by the pope in which participants took pilgrimage vows, wore crosses, and received a Crusade indulgence, which promised the remission of their sins and protection of their rights and property in their absence. Note that Crusades were never explicitly tied to Jerusalem; in the first century of the Crusading movement, Crusader armies fought everywhere from Spain to the Baltic, all explicitly with the same benefits as Crusaders going to Jerusalem.

While no king had joined the First Crusade, the Second Crusade was led by the monarchs of France and the Holy Roman Empire. These monarchs almost came to battle with Alexius's grandson, and each side blamed the other for the fact that the crusaders were defeated by the Turks crossing Anatolia. The two armies, greatly weakened, did make it to the kingdom of Jerusalem, where instead of retaking Edessa, they decided to attack the neutral city of Damascus. The failure of that assault led Damascus to join forces with the ruler of Aleppo and Mosul against the Crusaders, who sent **Saladin,** a Sunni Kurdish general, to conquer Fatimid Egypt. Once in control of the country, he reestablished the spiritual authority of the caliph of Baghdad and sent the Shia caliph into exile. From there he usurped the throne of his former Turkish lord and united the bulk of modern Egypt, Jordan, and Syria against the Crusaders. He defeated the armies of the Crusader states in 1187 at the battle of Hattin and retook Jerusalem a few months later. Saladin then began a campaign to conquer all the fortified Crusader strongholds along the Mediterranean coast.

The last of these Crusader cities standing was the city of Tyre, which was saved by the fortuitous arrival of an Italian vassal of and cousin to the Holy Roman Emperor named **Conrad of Montferrat**, who briefly became the nominal king of Jerusalem. He held the city until the main armies of the Third Crusade, led by King **Richard the Lionheart** of England, **Philip II** of France, and Holy Roman Emperor **Frederick Barbarossa**, arrived in the Holy Land. Frederick drowned in his march overland, and little of his army made it to Jerusalem. Meanwhile Richard and Philip, bitter rivals in Europe, found it nearly impossible to work together in the Holy Land. Shortly after retaking the key port of Acre, Philip left for home, citing illness. Richard valiantly fought on against Saladin, retaking the Crusaders' coastal cities and fortresses. Yet he was unable to retake Jerusalem, due largely to the machinations of Philip, who was trying desperately to usurp Richard's feudal holdings in France in his absence. This forced Richard, undefeated in the field, to sign a truce with Saladin and return home in 1192.

For the next decade, popes tried to organize Crusades to retake the Holy Land. In 1197, Frederick Barbarossa's son died just as his Crusade was getting underway. Its main legacy was more ill will with the Greeks, as he extorted a small fortune from the Greek emperor to finance the Crusade. Likewise, the endless wars between Richard the Lionheart and Philip II kept them and their vassals from joining the fight. However, a new pope, **Innocent III**, was elected in January 1198 and immediately began planning for a new Crusade. Like the First Crusade, it would be a Crusade not of kings but of the mid-tier nobility. His first three great recruits were from northern French families with deep ties to Crusading. **Thibault of Champagne**, the new Crusade's first leader, was the son of the previous king of Jerusalem. **Baldwin of Flanders** had perhaps the most illustrious Crusading pedigree in all of Europe, with ancestors who had distinguished themselves on the three previous Crusades. Meanwhile, **Louis of Blois** was out for redemption and to erase the stain of his great-grandfather's infamous desertion of the First Crusade. Louis's father had tried to undo that legacy by joining the Third Crusade but died before he could see battle.

Previous Crusades had a simple strategy: march or sail to the Holy Land and then launch a direct assault on Jerusalem. The planners of the Fourth Crusade, however, had a different target in mind: Egypt. Egypt was the richest and most strategic spot in the Middle East; it controlled the fertile Nile Delta and the trade routes between North Africa and the Middle East. It was also the power base for Saladin's successors, the Ayyubid dynasty, and it was through controlling Egypt that they held Jerusalem. By first conquering Egypt, the Crusaders would make the reconquest of Jerusalem possible. Because it would be impossible to launch a direct land assault on Egypt, the leaders of this Crusade needed a naval force large enough to transport a Crusader army of 33,500 men to Egypt.

The only nations with a naval force of that size were the Italian trading city-states. Since a war between Genoa and Pisa left their navies otherwise preoccupied, the only city-state able to fill the need was Venice. A deal was negotiated with **Enrico Dandolo**, the blind **doge** of Venice, who was by that point in his nineties. Despite his advanced age, he was shrewd and active. The number of ships required to carry the Crusaders absorbed almost the entire Venetian fleet and entailed the construction of many new ships as well; moreover, it required the suspension of practically all commercial activity for over a year. In exchange for their enormous commitment, the Venetians exacted an enormous price. The Venetians were made full partners in the Fourth Crusade and were entitled to half of all the profits of the Crusade. Furthermore, the Venetians would be richly compensated for the costs of transportation: 85,000 marks, double the annual income of the kings of England or France. The Crusaders agreed to this deal and set the departure date for early summer 1202.

By the time the deal was finalized, the prospective leader of the Crusade, Thibault of Champagne, had died at the age of twenty-two. His marshal, **Geoffrey of Villehardouin**, found a replacement as he returned from making the deal with Venice. Spending Christmas at the German imperial court, Villehardouin met **Marquis Boniface of Montferrat**. Boniface ruled a small principality in the Italian Alps north of Genoa, but his family had ties across the Mediterranean. He had succeeded his elder brothers, both of whom had played an active role in Greek politics. One brother, Renier, had been the regent in Constantinople for the boy-emperor Alexius II and the lover of the empress dowager. To cement ties to the West, Alexius was married to Agnes, the young daughter of the king of France, who was renamed Anna in the Greek fashion. For his services as regent, Renier was supposed to be invested with the lands around Thessalonica. Unlike in Western Europe, however, where lands were given as fiefs, in the East land was granted to important vassals through a system known as

pronoia. Here it was not the land given but the income from the taxes collected in the region that were granted for life and would then return to the emperor after death. This allowed an emperor to reward new men each generation and not be locked into ties with one family.

However, Andronicus Comnenus, a trouble-making older relative of the Byzantine emperor, returned from exile, killed Renier and Emperor Alexius II, and forcefully married the twelve-year old empress Anna, more than fifty years his junior. His reign descended into terror as he massacred all the Latin residents of Constantinople and ordered the arrest and execution of any Greek nobleman who could possibly oppose him. Yet, one nobleman finally stood up, Isaac Angelus, a descendant of one of Emperor Alexius I's daughters. Isaac killed the official sent to arrest him and rallied the people to his cause. The people declared him emperor, deposed Andronicus, and then paraded him through the streets in shame, his body ripped apart by his own subjects.

Emperor Isaac II Angelus was a capable monarch, and he managed the tense situation with Frederick Barbarossa and the Third Crusade well enough, but his heavy taxes caused a revolt by the Bulgarians, who demanded independence from the emperor. Isaac also had the help of another of Boniface's brothers, Conrad of Montferrat, who married the emperor's sister and put down a revolt by a Greek general named Alexius Branas. Anti-Latin sentiment against Conrad flared after he celebrated his victory by playing a drunken game of football with the head of the defeated general in the palace's great hall. Shortly after his victory, Conrad left for Jerusalem, where he saved Tyre and was appointed king of Jerusalem before being assassinated.

Isaac would be undone by his own brother, Alexius, whom he had ransomed from captivity and given rich lands and titles. Alexius led a coup against Isaac and seized the crown while his brother was away hunting. Once he returned, Isaac was officially deposed and was blinded, thus making him ineligible for the throne by Byzantine law. Isaac was then locked in a monastery in Constantinople, and his eldest son, Prince Alexius, was made a virtual prisoner at court. **Emperor Alexius III Angelus** tried to cement his power by being extremely generous to the nobles who had supported his takeover, but this and his failure to deal with the ongoing Bulgarian revolt led to the virtual bankruptcy of the empire. Then one day when Alexius III was hunting, Prince Alexius fled to the West onboard a Pisan ship, only to meet Villehardouin and Boniface at the now-famous Christmas dinner in 1201.

As the agreed-upon departure date of summer 1202 approached, the Crusade began to form up. Many Crusaders left their homes in Northern Europe after Easter and marched across France and Italy with their lords to meet up in Venice. However, only 12,000 of the predicted 33,500 men actually arrived in Venice. Since the costs of transportation were supposed to be paid on arrival by the Crusaders themselves, this left the Crusade's leaders 34,000 marks in debt to the Venetians. The Venetians refused to set sail until they were paid. As a result, it appeared that the Fourth Crusade would be over before it even started. At the end of the summer, Doge Dandolo agreed to set out immediately and to work out the financial obligations later, but only if the Crusade captured and then spent the winter at the Christian city of **Zara**, which had traditionally been a Venetian vassal but had recently offered itself as a vassal of the king of Hungary. Zara was captured, but the prospect of an army of Crusaders attacking Christians outraged a number of French Crusaders, who left the army. Pope Innocent III also responded by excommunicating the Venetian Crusaders, a fact kept secret from the rank and file Venetians on the Crusade.

Still in enormous debt, the exiled Prince Alexius Angelus reached out to the Crusaders with a solution to their problems. If they would put him on the throne of Byzantium, Alexius would pay the Crusaders 200,000 marks, provide 10,000 Byzantine soldiers for the Crusade, provision the entire

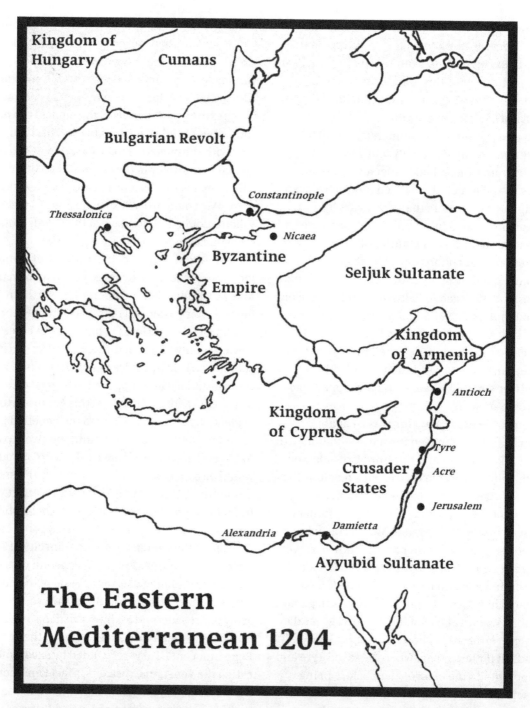

MAP 2 The Eastern Mediterranean in 1204, created by John and Amanda Giebfried.

Crusade, and provide a permanent force of knights to stay and defend Jerusalem after the Crusade ended. Alexius made one further offer: he promised to end the schism of 1054 and bring the Eastern Orthodox Church back under papal control. This offer sealed the bargain; the Crusaders now had a religious reason to go to Constantinople and not just a political one. Thus, out of practicality and faith, a Crusade to Egypt had become a Crusade that went first to Constantinople.

On June 24, 1203, exactly one year after departing Venice, the Crusaders reached Constantinople. Emperor Alexius III knew that the Crusaders were coming, but he made no military preparations; he even sold off most of the Byzantine navy for scrap parts. The Crusaders landed on the shore across from the city, and after diplomacy failed, they crossed the Bosporus. The Greek garrison under Alexius III marched out to meet them in battle. As a usurper, Alexius did not command much respect from his troops, and when the two armies clashed, the Byzantine army quickly retreated. The Crusaders had won. Not only did Alexius III flee the battlefield, but he also fled the city. The previous emperor, Isaac II, was restored to power, and his son, Prince Alexius, was declared co-emperor (now known as Alexius IV Angelus). The first order of business was to meet with the Crusaders. The Crusader leaders sent Geoffrey of Villehardouin to a private meeting with the emperors on July 18, 1203, in which Villehardouin insisted that the promises made by Alexius be fulfilled quickly so the Crusaders could continue speedily on to Egypt. Isaac, not knowing what his son had promised, was horrified by the scale of the concessions and thought it might be impossible for them to deliver everything required. This fear would turn out to be well-founded. When Alexius and Isaac informed the Orthodox Church hierarchy of their promise to submit to papal authority, there was immediate dissension; when this plan leaked out to the population of Constantinople, the people almost rose in rebellion. Worse, the emperors were forced to liquidate church assets and even melt down icons to pay the Crusaders because they didn't have enough money at hand, thanks to the lavish spending of Alexius III. Finally, on August 19, overzealous Crusaders set fire to one of the city's mosques. The fire soon spread to the surrounding area. Within three days, perhaps a third of all the homes in Constantinople had been burned. By January 1204, anti-Crusader tensions in Constantinople had reached a boiling point. Finally, a Byzantine nobleman, Alexius Ducas, who was also known as **Murtzuphlus**, took action. He kidnapped and murdered Emperor Alexius IV and then had himself crowned emperor at the Hagia Sophia. Murtzuphlus declared war on the Crusader army. Constantinople had been besieged seventeen times before in its 900-year history, but no previous enemy had ever breached the walls. The army of the Fourth Crusade had to decide if they were going to take a chance.

Part Three

THE GAME

Overview of Game Structure

1. **Debate on Attack and on "the Two Swords"**
Students will discuss whether the Crusade should attack Constantinople or whether it should leave the city behind and continue on toward Jerusalem. If the Crusade chooses to go to Jerusalem, it will skip the steps below and go to an alternate endgame. If the students decide to attack Constantinople, they must then decide how the Byzantine Empire should be reorganized after the city is captured. Because this would be a large undertaking, students must create an agreement (the "March Pact") on how to begin remaking Byzantium after their (hoped for) conquest.

2. **Siege and Sack of Constantinople**
Students will work together to take Constantinople and then make individual decisions of how to react when given a chance to sack the city.

3. **Remaking Byzantium**
Students will put in place the plans laid out in their March Pact, such as electing a new emperor, and thereafter see how successful their new empire will be.

RULES AND PROCEDURES

Objectives and Victory Conditions

Students achieve victory in this game both through individual achievements and through working together with their teammates to achieve their faction's objectives. Individual achievements are measured through the change in their *fama*, or influence points, described below. Faction objectives are listed on each of the faction overview sheets. Students may receive bonus points based on their achievements at the discretion of their instructor.

Fama (Influence Points)

The Fourth Crusade was made up of individuals who could assert their authority over the course of events to different degrees. Influence points, or to use a medieval term, *fama*, model this difference in power. Fama points are the currency of this game; each character starts with between one and ten points, but every player can gain points by delivering captivating speeches or developing cunning plans (as awarded by the game master), through character actions during the siege and sack of Constantinople, and by being awarded relics, titles and fiefs after the conquest of Constantinople. Five points of fama are awarded at the end of the game to members of the faction that achieves the largest number of its objectives as listed on its character sheet. Likewise, five additional fama points can be won by achieving the secret individual objective listed on a student's character sheet.

Fama points let players push forward their agendas. A student can spend a point of fama to gain an extra vote in any group decision or to reroll dice during an attack on the city. Once a point is spent, a character's point total permanently decreases.

At the end of the game, the player or players who increase their point totals the most are declared the winners and, at the discretion of their instructor, may be awarded bonus points on their final grade.

Money and Nefas

In addition to fama, there are two other scores. The first is money, which is measured in marks of silver. Every character begins with no money on hand, as a testament to the poverty of the crusade and its leaders. However, through certain game events, mostly the sacking of Constantinople, player can acquire large quantities of money. Money can be donated or traded between players, either publicly or privately (however, the game master must be informed about every such transaction). One hundred marks of silver can be cashed in with the game master anytime to gain one influence point.

Just as individuals can obtain fama, the Crusader army as a whole can obtain *nefas*, the Latin term for a violation of divine law. Nefas points are earned by committing actions that transgress acceptable medieval rules of conduct, such as murdering noncombatants or desecrating holy places. The Crusade's nefas score increases as a result of both collective decisions by the Crusade leadership and individual players' actions, especially during an attack on Constantinople. The Crusade's nefas score in part helps determine if the Greeks will work with the Crusaders once the Crusade comes to an end.

Gameplay

In the first phase of the game, the characters meet together in a council of war. This takes place in the Crusader camp in the town of Galata, located across the Golden Horn from Constantinople. As leader of the Fourth Crusade, Marquis Boniface of Montferrat presides over that meeting. He moderates the debate and makes sure that members of each faction get a chance to speak.

During phase 1, every player should be given a chance to express an opinion on whether or not to attack Constantinople, and only after due deliberations should the Marquis call for a vote. When debating the March Pact, each character may present issues they wish to be discussed during the deliberations. These speakers may make specific proposals for measures to include, which after debate can be added to the March Pact. Once everyone has had a chance to add and discuss their proposals, there will be a debate on the wording of the final document, which needs the support of a majority of players, including one member of each faction.

The rules for a siege and sack are described in the instructor's handbook and will be explained to students if they decide to attack the city—as are the steps that take place if the city is taken.

Major Issues for Debate

Like any important political choice, the decisions the Crusaders outside Constantinople face have huge long-term consequences. Medieval thinkers saw the intention and the result of an act as being indelibly linked, so they often thought out their actions in the long term. The leaders of the Crusades did the same. There are many issues that face the army, but they boil down to three key questions: (1) Should the Crusaders attack Constantinople and install a regime favorable to Crusading and the reconquest of the Holy Land, and if so, how? (2) How should secular authority be managed and constituted in a new Latin Empire? (3) How should religious issues be resolved in the same new empire?

Each of these major questions has a number of subquestions that could be asked and debated. Depending on your schedule and your instructor, you may have separate days for each of these subquestions, you may choose some but not others, or you may debate each question in one big block. No matter which way you choose, it's important to remember that medieval thinkers would have seen all these issues as linked to their core questions.

SHOULD THE CRUSADERS ATTACK CONSTANTINOPLE?

The question of whether the Crusade should attack Constantinople is a difficult one that has embedded in it two important questions in their own right.

1. Does the attack on Constantinople constitute a just war?

The question of what is and what is not a "just war" in Christian teaching has a long history, dating back to the earliest Christian thinkers, especially St. Augustine. It has also been debated by legal scholars, such as the great canon lawyer Gratian, who lived half a century before the Fourth Crusade. Students should read the documents in the sourcebook below and collectively decide what criteria make a war just and whether a proposed attack on Constantinople could be considered just.

2. Is an attack on Constantinople justifiable for a Crusader army?

While scholars had almost a millennium to debate the principles of just war, the idea of the Crusade had barely been around for a century in 1204. Before deciding on whether or not to attack, students will also have to determine what makes a Crusade and what actions are justifiable by the terms of their Crusading vow. This is not the first time the Crusade has had this debate. It played out before Zara in the winter of 1202-1203, with many Crusaders leaving the army in disgust. Now the question must be settled before there is a final decision on whether or not the city shall be attacked.

Should the army decide that an attack on Constantinople would be both a just war and a legitimate Crusading activity, it can attack without delay, but only under conditions agreed upon by the army as a whole. It must also consider the rules of engagement for such an attack. If the army decides that an attack would neither be a just war nor a legitimate Crusading activity, it must leave the city without launching an attack. Should the crusade decide it is one, but not the other, it may attack Constantinople.

3. How should the army attack?

The Fourth Crusade is an army of God on a mission to free the lands in which Christ once walked and liberate Eastern Christians from Muslim rule. The Crusaders are also bound to certain rules set up over the centuries by councils of Christian clerics to limit violence against those whom soldiers have a duty to protect. Yet the rules of war and the realities of the current situation are difficult to balance. The Crusaders must determine what the ground rules for any attack on Constantinople should be. Do you protect unarmed men, women, children, and clerics? What can be seized in a sack? Should the material and spiritual wealth found in Constantinople's churches be fair game?

Finally, if Constantinople falls, the Crusaders must determine what to do next. Should their first priority be the stability of their newly conquered empire, or should it be continuing on to Jerusalem as quickly as possible? Is it better to wait a few years to stabilize their conquests around the Aegean, or must they prioritize fulfilling their vows to liberate the Holy Land?

THE TWO SWORDS DOCTRINE

The doctrine of the two swords was first posed by Pope Gelasius I (492-496) and expanded by later medieval thinkers as a way to balance power between secular rulers, who, wielding the material sword, had the ability and the charge to led armies and maintain order, and the religious leaders of Christendom, wielding the spiritual sword, who were responsible for shepherding the faithful to the kingdom of heaven. While Gelasius used this distinction to assert his authority over an emperor, it was later used to justify church leaders' claims of control over larger political questions. While this distinction is mostly a legal one, it is also a useful way to group the series of issues under debate.

The Material Sword

If the Crusaders decide to attack Constantinople, they will need to grapple with important issues about the differences between leadership and political control in the East and West and lay out a plan to create a new empire under Crusader rule. Collectively, these issues about administering such political and organizational matters fall under the remit of the "material sword," since they do not deal with spiritual matters. Although religious leaders might point to these as being less important, because they do not directly impact the immortal souls of the participants in the Crusade, they would certainly acknowledge that these factors could greatly influence the success of the Crusade as a whole. Below are several important discussions that the Crusade leaders must reach a consensus on before they can attempt to attack the city.

1. Leadership

Who should be chosen to lead, and when should the choice be made? Should the Crusaders choose one of their own as the new emperor, or should they pick a Greek emperor or empress who will work with the Crusaders? They must also decide if it is better to elect an emperor before the conquest or to wait until after the city falls. Moreover, they must decide if this new emperor should have all the powers a Byzantine emperor traditionally holds, or if that power should be more limited.

2. Land Organization

The Greeks have traditionally organized their empire into military provinces, or *themes*, and granted blocks of tax revenues to nobles in a system known as *pronoia*. This is radically different from the Western European feudal system which the crusaders are familiar with. Therefore, they must debate the relative merits of both systems and decide if the empire should be reorganized on feudal principles or maintained in its current form.

3. Trade Policy

Constantinople is the largest city in the Christian world and a global trade hub for goods coming from as far away as China. Italian and other Western merchants have come to trade in the city for centuries, and over the years they have obtained rights and privileges there. The most generous arrangement was given to Venice as a traditional ally of the emperors of Constantinople. As a major part of this Crusade, Venetian Crusaders will almost certainly want to see these rights continued and even expanded. You must determine to what extent these requests should be granted.

The Spiritual Sword

While there are many small differences between political rule in the East and the West, the most obvious gulf between the Byzantine Empire and the kingdoms from where the Crusaders hail is a cluster of religious differences. Even though political leaders might be less well-versed in these debates, their religiosity is not in question. Every Crusader has a direct spiritual connection to the campaign; Crusades are, at their heart, penitential armed pilgrimages. Although the "spiritual sword" appears to have a less immediate impact on the progress of the Crusade, it is nevertheless at the core of the whole movement. There are many facets to this debate that matter a great deal to religious officials, without whose support the Crusade could not succeed.

RESOLVING THE SCHISM

Since 1054, the churches of Rome and Constantinople have not recognized each other as legitimate, and the Christian world has been divided. Now this Crusade has a chance to end the schism and reunite the Christian world. However, the Crusaders will first have to decide on whose terms that union will take place and determine to what degree the Greeks should be able to maintain their historical, theological, and liturgical differences from the Latin West. Must they acknowledge that the pope in Rome is the head of the universal church and accept the Western position on theological issues such as the wording of the Nicene Creed? Must they also accept Western liturgical practices such as the use of unleavened bread in the Eucharist or even the use of Latin as the language of the Mass? Finally, who should be patriarch in Constantinople—a Crusader cleric, a Greek churchman, or perhaps even one of each?

Assignments and Grading

Your instructor will give you detailed instructions on what is expected from you as part of playing this game. Most will require you to participate fully in the game by making two to three formal speeches from the podium in character or other similarly important presentations. Such a speech will show your ability to construct an argument based in the primary sources found in this book.

You may also be required to write a pair of papers after the game is completed reflecting on the success or failure of your class's version of the

Fourth Crusade and how that informs your understanding of the course of the historical Fourth Crusade. You may also complete additional or alternative assignments, as assigned by your instructor. The two suggested topics are described below.

Here is the prompt for the first topic: With the exception of the First Crusade, no military campaign of the entire Middle Ages spawned more histories than the Fourth Crusade. The reason for this is simple: Crusaders returning home with relics and treasures from a conquered Christian city needed to explain exactly why they did what they did. This genre in medieval literature is known as the *apologia*. It is a formal defense of one's actions and beliefs and should not be confused with the modern use of "apology" as an expression of regret. After finishing the game, you will write a four-to-five-page apologia telling the history of the Crusade from your perspective, defending your actions and those of your faction, and assigning credit and blame for the success or failure of the Crusade.

In upper-level courses or seminars you may also write a second postgame paper: a five-to-seven-page analysis of the failure of the historical Fourth Crusade, as informed by the sources in the primary source appendix provided as a handout by instructors. While reflecting on your own choices in the game, try to isolate the key factors and turning points that led to the eventual collapse of the Crusade. Also, grapple with the question of what a "successful" Fourth Crusade would even look like in history.

Part Four

ROLES AND FACTIONS

Factions

Most students in game will play characters aligned with one of four factions. These players will work together with the members of their faction to achieve shared goals. While all factions are working together to ensure the overall success of the Crusade, they also are competing with each other to lead the Crusade and shape its agenda.

The Northern French faction represents a group of Crusading lords who rule lands in northwestern France and what is today Belgium, and they share the same French language and culture. This is the largest faction in the game, as it represents the largest single group of Crusaders in the army.

The Imperial faction is made up of Crusaders who come from the Holy Roman Empire, which covers both the lands of medieval Germany and most of northern Italy. The members of this faction are very diverse; they are led by an Italian, Marquis Boniface of Montferrat, but include Germans and others loyal to the imperial cause. They are nevertheless a minority in terms of men on the Crusade—more Northern French and Venetians have come on this expedition. Despite that, it is the marquis who was chosen as the Crusade's leader and who will lead the proceedings of the War Council that comprises the game's initial setting.

The Venetian faction represents the Crusaders from the city of Venice. They joined the Crusade as partners to provide transportation and naval support to the Northern French and Imperial crusaders. They are led by their doge, Enrico Dandolo, who is over ninety years old and totally blind. However, he is an effective and charismatic leader for the Crusade. Venice is very different from the other Crusader homelands both because it is a republic and because its residents have traditionally made their living as sailors and merchants, not as soldiers and farmers.

Unlike the other three factions, the Clerical faction is made up of characters from all across medieval Europe. What binds them together is a common calling in life—to be priests of God—as well as a shared loyalty to the pope. While they all have taken vows of poverty, the members of this faction are still very powerful men with great resources and influence. Some are bishops, who rule whole dioceses and collaborate with the papacy to run the church in their parts of the world. Others are powerful abbots of Cistercian monasteries that control large land holdings rivalling those of secular lords. This faction is meant to be the conscience and the spiritual compass for the Crusade. While other factions worry about power and getting ahead in this world, the Clerical faction must make sure that the souls of the Crusaders make their way to heaven.

Indeterminates

Some characters do not belong to any faction. These players are called indeterminates. They represent different regions, social classes, and experiences from those represented by the four factions. They are also free agents, able to support any faction they feel supports their interests and the interests of the Crusade overall. They may join any faction at any time or may remain free from factional entanglements. The choice is up to them; however, once they join a faction, they must remain part of that faction until the end of the game. They also can win bonus fama should that faction achieve more of its objectives than its rivals do.

Character Biographies

Not all characters may be in your simulation, since the number of students and the focus of your course may vary at your game master's discretion.

NORTHERN FRENCH FACTION

Baldwin of Flanders. Count Baldwin IX of Flanders and Hainaut is the king's brother-in-law and one of the most powerful lords in all of France. Baldwin took the cross with his much-beloved wife, Marie of Champagne, on Ash Wednesday in the year 1200. He comes from a long line of Crusaders going back to the First Crusade. He brings with him on Crusade an army bigger than that of any other leader.

Louis of Blois. Count Louis of Blois is a young, ambitious, and powerful count related to the royal houses of both France and England. His lands in Blois are just west of Paris, and his family has always included among the most important lords in the kingdom.

Hugh of Saint-Pol. Count Hugh of Saint-Pol is the oldest of the Northern French lords on the Crusade. He is a veteran of the Third Crusade, where he distinguished himself at the siege of Acre. Although nominally a vassal of the Count of Flanders, he is a great count in his own right and a voice of experience to the younger lords.

Geoffrey of Villehardouin. Lord Geoffrey of Villehardouin, Marshal of Champagne, was the military adviser and right-hand man to the young Count Thibaut of Champagne, the first leader of the Fourth Crusade. He negotiated the Treaty of Venice, which made the Venetians partners in the Crusade, and when Thibaut died he was instrumental in finding Boniface of Montferrat as his replacement. He serves as the de facto leader of the knights from Champagne and an elder statesman of the Crusade.

Henry of Flanders. Henry of Flanders, Lord of Harlebeke and Biervliet, is the ambitious unmarried younger brother of Count Baldwin of Flanders. He is his elder brother's best general and his closest confidant. Yet as the third son of Count Baldwin VIII, he was only granted two very minor lordships in the West, leaving him to look East to the Crusade as a chance to make his name and fortune.

Conon of Bethune. Conon of Bethune is a knight and the younger brother of the Lord of Bethune. He is also an acclaimed troubadour.

Peter of Amiens. Peter, Lord of Amiens, is a respected vassal of Count Hugh of Saint-Pol. His father died on the Third Crusade, and his mother remarried the brother of Count Hugh; thus, Peter is Count Hugh's nephew as well.

Milo of Brebant. Milo of Brebant is the son of the marshal of the County of Champagne and an experienced diplomat.

James of Avesnes. James of Avesnes is a vassal of Count Baldwin of Flanders and a capable, if underexperienced, diplomat.

Peter of Bracieux. Peter of Bracieux is the lord of Bracieux, a small fief near Beauvais in Clermont, making him a vassal of Count Louis of Blois. He is respected as one of the bravest knights of the Crusade.

Baldwin of Beauvoir. Baldwin of Beauvoir is a French knight from around Cambrai in the county of Hainaut and a vassal of Count Baldwin.

Eustace of Flanders. Eustace of Flanders is the illegitimate younger brother of Baldwin and Henry of Flanders.

IMPERIAL FACTION

Boniface of Montferrat. Boniface, Marquis of Montferrat was the leader of the Fourth Crusade a great lord of the Holy Roman Empire in Italy, ruling the lands between Genoa and the Italian Alps. He was a close ally of the last Holy Roman Emperor, Henry VI, and now serves his brother, the uncrowned king, Philip of Swabia. Philip's brother-in-law was Alexius IV, and Boniface played a large role in diverting the crusade to Constantinople to put prince Alexius on the Byzantine throne. This was not the first Eastern adventure for Boniface's family. His elder brother Conrad was king of Jerusalem and was married to a Byzantine princess and another brother, Renier, was the regent for the Byzantine Emperor Alexius II and was awarded the kingdom of Thessalonica.

Oberto of Biandrate. Count Oberto II of Biandrate was an Italian count loyal to the Holy Roman Emperors. His family had a long tradition of crusading, dating back to the First Crusade. He was also a close ally and cousin of Boniface of Montferrat.

Berthold of Katzenellenbogen. Count Berthold of Katzenellenbogen is an ethnically German count from the Southern Rhineland. He is a partisan loyal to both King Philip of Swabia and Boniface of Montferrat.

Raimbaut of Vaqueiras. Raimbaut of Vaqueiras is a troubadour from Provence in southern France. He is in the employ of Boniface of Montferrat, for whom he has written several songs and an epic poem of praise.

William of Arles. William of Arles is the viscount of Marseilles and Boniface's marshal.

Raveno della Carceri. Raveno della Carceri is a knight loyal to Boniface who comes from the area around Verona in Northern Italy and is an intermediary between his faction and Venice.

Guido Pallavicini. Guido Pallavicini is the marquis of Scipione and controls a number of fiefs in northern Italy between Parma and Piacenza. He is a loyal follower of the imperial family.

Henry of Ulmen. Henry of Ulmen is a knight from western Germany with a great devotion to relics.

VENETIAN FACTION

Enrico Dandolo. Doge Enrico Dandolo of Venice was elected leader of Venice in 1192. Now aged ninety, and blind for several decades, he is the oldest and perhaps the shrewdest and most respected man in Venice. He comes from a respected Venetian family and is a skilled ambassador for Venice. During his reign he has reformed Venetian coinage and brought Venice into the Fourth Crusade as a full partner with the French and Imperial Crusaders.

Angelo Falier. Angelo Falier is a nobleman from one of Venice's most famous families and holds the prestigious post of procurator of Saint Mark's Basilica in Venice.

Pantaleone Barbo. Pantaleone Barbo is a wealthy Venetian nobleman who has joined in the Fourth Crusade.

Marino Zeno. Marino Zeno is a Venetian merchant with ties to the Venetian community in Constantinople.

Pietro Steno. Pietro Steno is a common Venetian sailor on the Fourth Crusade from the parish of St. Simon the Prophet in Venice. He is also a successful businessman and owns land on the island of Torcello, north of Venice.

Matteo Steno. Matteo Steno is the very religious uncle of Pietro Steno. A man of substantial means, he is aware of but not involved in his nephew's schemes.

Marco Sanudo. Marco Sanudo is the nephew of Doge Enrico Dandolo and a Venetian nobleman and ship captain.

Marino Ballaresso. Marino Ballaresso is a Venetian nobleman and diplomat.

Andrea Balduino. Andrea Balduino is a common Venetian sailor on the Fourth Crusade from the parish of St. Simon the Prophet in Venice and a friend of Pietro Steno.

Andrew Valero. Andrew Valero is a Venetian knight-commander who is helping to lead the army attached to the Venetian fleet.

Domenico of Constantinople. Domenico is a Venetian resident of Constantinople. He has established interests in the city and contacts with the Byzantine government, most notably the historian and bureaucrat Nicetas Choniates.

CLERICAL FACTION

Nivelon of Soissons. Nivelon of Chérizy was made bishop of Soissons in Picardy in 1175. He is the longest serving of any of the bishops on the Crusade and therefore, in the absence of a papal legate (who has gone ahead to the Holy Land), is the de facto spiritual leader of the Fourth Crusade.

Conrad of Halberstadt. Conrad of Krosigk, Bishop of Halberstadt, is a powerful bishop in the Holy Roman Empire. His see is in Halberstadt, a city in Saxony. He was elected in 1201 and took the cross a year later. He is a leader, both religious and temporal, of many German Crusaders.

Martin of Parisis. Abbot Martin of Parisis is an established Cistercian abbot from the borderlands of France and Germany.

Peter of Luciendo. Abbot Peter of Luciendo is a great Cistercian abbot in Lombardy and a close ally of Boniface of Montferrat.

John of Noyon. John Faicete was born in the city of Noyon. He served as the chancellor of Flanders under Count Baldwin IX and his father and later was appointed by the pope as bishop of Acre in the Holy Land.

Garnier of Troyes. Garnier of Trainel, Bishop of Troyes, is a powerful cleric in Champagne whose fortunes have fallen dramatically over his reign, particularly since his cathedral burned to the ground.

Peter of Bethlehem. Peter of Bethlehem was a cleric from the Holy Roman Empire who was chosen by Pope Innocent III to be the bishop of Bethlehem. He has joined the Crusade to retake his post.

Hugh of Saint-Ghislain. Abbot Hugh of Saint-Ghislain rules the ancient Benedictine abbey of Saint-Ghislain in Hainaut.

Walon of Dampierre. Walon of Dampierre was born the son of a knight, Richard of Dampierre, but chose to become a priest. After being ordained he took up the post of a parish priest in the diocese of Langres in Burgundy.

Warin of Douai. Warin of Douai is a canon regular from the city of Douai in Flanders. He served at the church of St. Ame before joining the Crusade.

INDETERMINATES

Robert of Clari. Robert of Clari is a poor knight from Clari, part of the village of Pernois, near

Amiens in northern France. Owning just 6.5 hectares of land, he has enough to call himself a knight, but little else. He is a vassal of Peter of Amiens. Along with his brother Aleaumes, an armed cleric, he has joined the Fourth Crusade.

Empress Anna. Born as Princess Agnes of France and renamed when she came to Constantinople, Anna is the youngest daughter of King Louis VII of France. She came east as a young girl to marry the child-emperor Alexius II. Renier of Montferrat was her regent, but he was overthrown by the usurper Andronicus Commenus, who killed Alexius II and Renier and forced Agnes/Anna to marry him, even though he was fifty years older than her. As a politically valuable widow, she was not allowed to remarry by the Angelus emperors.

Theodore Branas. Theodore Branas is a powerful and pragmatic Byzantine general from the city of Adrianople who is out of favor with the Angelus emperors. His father led a rebellion against Isaac II, only to be killed and beheaded in battle by Conrad of Montferrat.

Brother Barozzi. Brother Barozzi is the commander of the Knights Templar in Lombardy.

Renier of Travele. Renier of Travele is a wealthy and powerful citizen of the Republic of Siena in Tuscany. He is also trained as a knight and owns four castles around Siena.

Odo of La Roche. Otto of La Roche is the lord of La-Roche-Sur-l'Ognon in Burgundy in southeastern France. His family has ruled the castle there for most of the last century, and as the most notable of all the Crusaders from Burgundy, he serves as an independent power base not tied to either the Northern French or Imperial Crusaders.

Amedeus Buffa. Also known as Amédée Pofey in French, Amadeus Buffa is a moderately well-off knight from around Geneva, Switzerland. He is a low-ranking knight fluent in French, German, and Italian who is willing to compromise for the good of the crusade.

Pierre Vidal. Pierre Vidal is a famous court troubadour from Provence in southern France. He worked across Europe for the counts of Toulouse and Montpellier in France; the kings of Aragon, Castile, and Leon in Spain; and he even accompanied Richard the Lionheart to the Holy Land on the Third Crusade.

Andrew of Ureboise. Andrew of Ureboise is a daring knight fighting in the household of Bishop Nivelon of Soissons.

King Lalibela of Ethiopia. King Lalibela is a powerful African ruler who is visiting Constantinople as part of a pilgrimage from Jerusalem to Constantinople to Rome. He is caught in the city at the moment of crisis, alongside his royal retinue.

Walframe of Gemona. Walframe of Gemona is a common Italian man who, although not a Venetian, is a resident of Venice and has chosen to join the Venetian fleet on the Fourth Crusade. He is a pious Christian who made his last will before heading off on Crusade.

Part Five

PRIMARY SOURCES

The following section contains the primary sources that you, your faction mates, and your colleagues will need to start the work of unravelling what you think about the key issues and what the best course of action might be. While each of the sections has a pertinent subtheme, all of these sources demonstrate the way that the wider discussion of the two swords doctrine widely permeated medieval thought. The balance between the immediate and political consequences of an action and its eternal and religious implications was constantly at work. Because of its pervasiveness, we have put the two swords letter from Pope Gelasius and the much later bull *Unam sanctam*, which provided a revised definition after the Crusading movement had its peak, in a separate section before the main sources. The main four sections below describe the Crusading movement as a whole, the way societies were ordered in the medieval world, the Republic of Venice (which was peculiar, even in its own time), and the specific disputes between Latin and Greek Rite Christianity. (Your instructor also has access to a dossier that includes extended extracts from three primary source narratives of the Fourth Crusade by eyewitnesses. These may be included or excluded in your preparations at the discretion of your instructor.) With all of these primary sources, pay careful attention to the way they relate to the two swords doctrine, and remember that medieval people were just as smart as modern people but had different vocabularies and value systems with which they expressed their ideas. Just as we can say one thing but mean another, so too did medieval people "code-switch" in powerful ways; primary sources are no exception.

Prefatory Sources

The Two Swords Letter of Gelasius and Unam Sanctam

In the sections of this chapter that follow these first two primary sources, you will see a wide range of issues expressed and debated by contemporary figures. Crusading, from its very origins, was a kind of hybrid: a pilgrimage for the penitent and a war that was, in theory, free from sin. Its representation of the natural partnership between religious authority and material politics was, for all intents and purposes, unique in the medieval world. The core of this hybridization, however, was an understanding of the world as being divided between what St. Augustine of Hippo termed "the two cities"—one, a city of man that was corrupt, imperfect, and sinful; the other, the city of God, which was inherently holy, sacralizing, and a rejection of the sinful present in expectation of an immortal and blessed future. In the two letters from this prefatory selection of sources, you will find the clearest expressions of this view in practical terms for political and religious organization. Effectively, the debates about secondary themes—such as the organization of the Crusade, the justness of holy war against Byzantium, or the proper ordering of religious doctrines—were symptoms of a much larger quarrel about which was more powerful: the secular authority or a religious one. It must be noted here, though, that the frequency with which religious leaders expressed the theoretical superiority of their position was inversely proportional to their practical superiority. Put differently, religious officials were supposed to be above political ones, but they rarely were, and they repeated their claims because they felt their authority slipping. We ought not to read these claims with a cynical perspective, however, since religious lenses were the primary determining perspective for viewing the world at large. Just as our own world has placed its confidences on the altar of electron microscopes and petri dishes, so too did medieval minds place their trust in the relics of saints and the prayers of the faithful.

1. LETTER OF POPE GELASIUS TO EMPEROR ANASTASIUS ON THE SUPERIORITY OF THE SPIRITUAL OVER TEMPORAL POWER (494)

The famous "two swords" letter of Pope Gelasius to Emperor Anastasius was one of the most important policy statements from late antiquity, and its influence persisted for nearly one thousand years (when it was given a facelift by Pope Boniface VIII). Expressing the differences between the spiritual (religious) authority of the papacy and the temporal (physical/worldly) authority of the emperor, Gelasius makes a careful argument for the importance of the emperor as the instrument of divine will, as interpreted by the papacy. Effectively subordinated to the pope, the emperor as presented here was given important duties but nevertheless was secondary to the bishop of Rome. While other sources in the sections below present a variety of perspectives on a number of constituent issues, the debates in this simulation are either iterations or refractions of this central question about the competing roles played by political and religious authority.

There are two powers, august Emperor, by which this world is chiefly ruled, namely, the sacred authority of the priests and the royal power. Of these, that of the priests is the more weighty, since they have to render an account for even the kings of men in the divine judgment. You are also aware, dear Son, that while you are permitted honorably to rule over humankind, yet in things divine you bow your head humbly before the leaders of the clergy and await from their hands the means of your salvation. In the reception and proper disposition of the heavenly mysteries, you recognize that you should be subordinate rather than superior to the religious order, and that in these matters you depend on their judgment rather than wish to force them to follow your will. If the ministers of religion, recognizing the supremacy granted you from heaven in matters affecting the public order, obey your laws, lest otherwise they might obstruct the course of secular affairs by irrelevant considerations, with what readiness should you not yield them obedience to whom is assigned the dispensing of the sacred mysteries of religion. Accordingly, just as there is no slight danger in the case of the priests if they refrain from speaking when the service of the divinity requires, so there is no little risk for those who disdain—which God forbid—when they should obey. And if it is fitting that the hearts of the faithful should submit to all priests in general who properly administer divine affairs, how much the more is obedience due to the bishop of that see which the Most High ordained to be above all others, and which is consequently dutifully honored by the devotion of the whole Church.

2. POPE BONIFACE VIII ON THE PRIMACY OF THE PAPACY (1302)

Although written later than the Fourth Crusade, Boniface VIII's letter on the primacy of the Roman Church represents the culmination and distillation of centuries of papal policy toward Christendom as a whole. Boniface argues for the importance of Rome as the spiritual head of the whole world, and underlines the ways in which Gelasius's two swords letter worked in practice. Thus, Boniface's letter can be interpreted as a kind of explanation of Gelasius's letter for the high medieval world and as a kind of expansive corollary for many of the key issues presented in the years after Gelasius's letter was issued.

Urged by faith, we are obliged to believe and to maintain that the Church is one, holy, catholic, and also apostolic. We believe in her firmly, and we confess with simplicity that outside of her there is neither salvation nor the remission of sins, as the Spouse in the Canticles [Sg 6:8] proclaims: "One is my dove, my perfect one. She is the only one, the chosen of her who bore her," and she represents one sole mystical body whose head is Christ and the head of Christ is God [1 Cor 11:3]. In her then is one Lord, one faith, one baptism [Eph 4:5]. There had been at the time of the deluge only one ark of Noah, prefiguring the one Church, which ark, having been finished to a single cubit, had only one pilot and guide—that is, Noah—and we read that, outside of this ark, all that subsisted on the earth was destroyed. We venerate this Church as one, the Lord having said by the mouth of the prophet: "Deliver, O God, my soul from the sword and my only one from the hand of the dog" [Ps 21:20]. He has prayed for his soul, that is, for himself, heart and body; and this body, that is to say, the Church, He has called one because of the unity of the Spouse, of the faith, of the sacraments, and of the charity of the Church. This is the tunic of the Lord, the seamless tunic, which was not rent but which was cast by lot [Jn 19:23-24].

Therefore, of the one and only Church there is one body and one head, not two heads like a monster—that is, Christ and the Vicar of Christ, Peter and the successor of Peter, since the Lord speaking to Peter Himself said, "Feed my sheep" [Jn 21:17], meaning my sheep in general, not these, nor those in particular, whence we understand that He entrusted all to him [i.e., Peter]. Therefore, if the Greeks or others should say that they are not confided to Peter and to his successors, they must confess not being the sheep of Christ, since Our Lord says in John, "There is one sheepfold and one shepherd."

We are informed by the texts of the gospels that in this Church and in its power are two swords, namely, the spiritual and the temporal. For when the Apostles say, "Behold, here are two swords" [Lk 22:38], that is to say, in the Church, since the Apostles were speaking, the Lord did not reply that there were too many, but sufficient. Certainly the one who denies that the temporal sword is in the power of Peter has not listened well to the word of the Lord commanding, "Put up thy sword into thy scabbard" [Mt 26:52]. Both, therefore, are in the power of the Church, that is to say, the spiritual and the material sword, but the former is to be administered for the Church but the latter by the Church; the former in the hands of the priest; the

latter by the hands of kings and soldiers, but at the will and sufferance of the priest. However, one sword ought to be subordinated to the other, and temporal authority subjected to spiritual power. For since the Apostle said, "There is no power except from God and the things that are, are ordained of God" [Rom 13:1-2], but they would not be ordained if one sword were not subordinated to the other and if the inferior one, as it were, were not led upwards by the other. For, according to the Blessed Dionysius, it is a law of the divinity that the lowest things reach the highest place by intermediaries. Then, according to the order of the universe, all things are not led back to order equally and immediately, but the lowest by the intermediary, and the inferior by the superior. Hence we must recognize the more clearly that spiritual power surpasses in dignity and in nobility any temporal power whatever, as spiritual things surpass the temporal. This we see very clearly also by the payment, benediction, and consecration of the tithes, but the acceptance of power itself and by the government even of things. For with truth as our witness, it belongs to spiritual power to establish the terrestrial power and to pass judgment if it has not been good. Thus is accomplished the prophecy of Jeremias concerning the Church and the ecclesiastical power: "Behold to-day I have placed you over nations, and over kingdoms" and the rest.

Therefore, if the terrestrial power err, it will be judged by the spiritual power; but if a minor spiritual power err, it will be judged by a superior spiritual power; but if the highest power of all err, it can be judged only by God, and not by man, according to the testimony of the Apostle: "The spiritual man judgeth of all things and he himself is judged by no man" [1 Cor 2:15]. This authority, however (though it has been given to man and is exercised by man), is not human but rather divine, granted to Peter by a divine word and reaffirmed to him (Peter) and his successors by the one whom Peter confessed, the Lord saying to Peter himself, "Whatsoever you shall bind on earth shall be bound also in heaven" etc. [Mt 16:19]. Therefore whoever resists this power thus ordained by God, resists the ordinance of God [Rom 13:2], unless he invent like Manicheus two beginnings, which is false and judged by us heretical, since according to the testimony of Moses, it is not in the beginnings but in the beginning that God created heaven and earth [Gen 1:1]. Furthermore, we declare, we proclaim, we define that it is absolutely necessary for salvation that every human creature be subject to the Roman pontiff.

Section One
Crusades and Just Wars

Armed conflict is as old as time itself, and over the centuries every major world religion has had to grapple with issues of legitimate and illegitimate forms of violence. Christianity, which emerged as an essentially pacifist religion, had to grapple with issues of war as it came to be the dominant faith in the Roman Empire. Thinkers such as St. Augustine of Hippo argued for the creation of a doctrine of "just war," which set out exactly when it was right for a Christian to fight and kill. This remained a fundamental principle that guided church-sanctioned violence in the Middle Ages. That changed with the coming of the Crusades, which provided a new framework for church-approved violence. The documents below describe how medieval authors understood the concepts of Crusade and just war in the context of their own times. In general, Crusading was one manner in which the spiritual sword could be understood as directing, guiding, shaping, or influencing the use of the material sword to achieve its religious goals; when soldiers vowed to fight and die to restore Jerusalem to Christian control, they were vowing to restore an inherently Christian worldview that benefitted the immortal souls of every Christian.

1. INNOCENT III'S CALLING OF THE FOURTH CRUSADE (1198)

The Fourth Crusade was called by Innocent III in 1198 as a response to the continuing growth of the Ayyubid dynasty's influence in the Near East. This papal bull, often referred to as *Post miserabile* according to the first Latin words of the body text, argues for attacking Jerusalem via an invasion of Egypt. Although this strategy was first proposed by Richard the Lionheart and was later employed by Louis IX of France, the preparation of a massive marine landing force required enormous resources. The immense outlay of military materiel was crucial to achieving the larger objective of recovering Jerusalem, and the importance of papal direction for the campaign cannot be overstated. Pope Innocent III laid out the religious reasoning for why this particular campaign could be considered a Crusade in a series of letters to archbishops across Europe. Below is the letter he sent to the archbishop of Narbonne in southern France.

To the archbishop of Narbonne and his suffragans, as well as the abbots, priors, and other prelates of churches, also to the counts, barons, and all the people residing in the province of Narbonne:

Part 1: The Theological Call to Arms

Following the pitiable collapse of the territory of Jerusalem, following the lamentable massacre of the Christian people, following the deplorable invasion of that land on which the feet of Christ had stood and where God, our King, had deigned, before the beginning of time, to work out salvation in the midst of the Earth, following the ignominious alienation from our possession of the vivifying Cross, on which the Salvation of the world hung and effaced the handwriting of former death, the Apostolic See, alarmed over the ill fortune of such calamity, grieved. It cried out and wailed to such a degree that due to incessant crying out, its throat was made hoarse, and from excessive weeping, its eyes almost failed. Indeed, it is true that, in the words of the prophet, had we forgotten Jerusalem our right hand would forget us: "Our tongue would stick to our palate, had we not remembered it." Still, the Apostolic See cries out, and like a trumpet it raises its voice, eager to arouse the Christian peoples to fight Christ's battle and to avenge the injury done to the Crucified One, employing the words of him who says, "O, all of you who pass along this way, behold and see if there is any sorrow like my sorrow." For behold, our inheritance has been turned over to strangers, our houses have gone to foreigners. The streets of Zion's mourn because there are none who come to the feast; her enemies have been placed in charge. The Sepulcher of the Lord, which the prophet foretold would be so glorious," has been profaned by the impious and made inglorious. Our glory, regarding

which the Apostle says, "I have no glory save in the Cross of our Lord Jesus Christ," is held in hostile hands, and Lord Jesus Christ Himself, who, by dying for us, took captive our captivity, as though taken captive by the impious, is driven into exile from His inheritance. In former days, when the ark of the Lord of Sabaoth resided in camp, Uriah refused to enter his house and even withheld himself from the licit embrace of his wife. Now, however, our princes, with the glory of Israel having been transferred from its place to our disgrace, give themselves over to adulterous embraces, thereby abusing luxuries and wealth. And while they harass one another in turn with inexorable hatred, while one strives to take vengeance on the other in return for his injuries, not one is moved by the injury done to the Crucified One. They pay no attention to the fact that our enemies now insult us, saying:

Where is your God, who can deliver neither Himself nor you from our hands? Behold! We now have profaned your holy places. Behold! We now have extended our hand to the objects of your desire, and in the initial assault we have violently overrun and hold, against your will, those places in which you pretend your superstition began. Already we have weakened and shattered the lances of the Gauls; we have frustrated the efforts of the English; we have now, for a second time, held in check the might of the Germans; we have tamed the proud Spaniards. And although you took steps to rouse up all your powers against us, you have, thus far, scarcely made progress in any way. Where, then, is your God? Let Him now rise up and help you, and let Him protect you and Himself. The Germans, indeed, who presumed they would gain an unheard of triumph over us, sailed over to our land in a spirit of impetuousness. And although they had taken the single stronghold of Beirut, when no one was defending it, except for the fact that fortuitous flight had delivered them (as well as your other lords), they would have woefully experienced our might against them, and their progeny would have bewailed in perpetuity their slaughter. And as for your kings and princes, whom we earlier drove out of the lands of the East, in order to conceal their timidity by a show of boldness, upon returning to their lurking-holes (we forbear saying "kingdoms"), they prefer to attack one another in turn rather than to experience once again our might and power.

What, therefore, remains, except that, after having cut down with an avenging sword those whom you abandoned when you ran away with the excuse that your lands needed looking after, we should launch an attack on your lands, for the purpose of effacing your name and memory? How, therefore, brothers and sons, are we to rebut the insults of insulters? How can we answer them, inasmuch as we see them, for their part, adhering to the truth, judging by the clear evidence that has recently reached our hearing? For we received a letter from the lands across the sea to the effect that, when the Germans reached Acre by ship, they seized the stronghold of Beirut, which was defended by no one. Meanwhile, the Saracens, attacking Jaffa across the way, gained possession of it by storm and razed it to the ground, after they had killed many thousands of Christians. On their part, the Germans, upon hearing rumors regarding the death of the emperor, embarked on returning ships at an unexpected time for passage. Upon this happening, the Saracens, who had assembled a large army to oppose them, rage to such a degree against Christian lands that the Christians can neither leave their cities without peril nor remain within them without terror. Indeed, the sword threatens them outside and dread within.

Therefore, take up, O sons, the spirit of fortitude; receive the shield of faith and the helmet of salvation. Trust not in numbers or in might but rather in the power of God, who has no difficulty saving with many or with few, and according to your respective means, come to the aid of Him

through whom you exist, live, and have being. Indeed, it was for you that He emptied Himself, accepting the form of a servant, was made in the form of a man and appeared in human likeness. He became obedient all the way to death—yes, the death of the Cross. And while He is poor, you enjoy abundance; while He is put to flight, you are at rest, and you aid neither the Pauper nor the Exile! Who, then, at a time of such exigency would refuse obedience to Jesus Christ? When he should come to stand before His tribunal for judgment, what could he say to Him by way of defending himself? If God submitted to death for humanity, will a human hesitate to submit to death for God, inasmuch as the sufferings of the moment are not comparable to the future glory that shall be revealed in us? Shall the servant also deny his Lord temporal riches when the Lord bestows on His servant eternal riches, which neither eye has seen nor ear heard, nor have they entered into the heart of man? Therefore, let a man store up treasures in Heaven, where thieves neither break in nor steal, where neither rust nor worms corrupt.

Part 2: The Practical Call to Arms
Therefore, let all and each make themselves ready so that next March, each and every city by itself, likewise counts and barons, in accordance with their respective means, might send forth a certain number of warriors at their own expense for the defense of the land of the Lord's birth, and there they are to remain at least two years. For, although we have continuous solicitude for all churches on a daily basis, yet still we count it as if special among our other cares that we very much desire with full zeal to aid the lands of the East. Otherwise, if it happens that help is delayed, the bruch (a kind of wingless grasshopper) might devour what the locust has left, and the latest state of affairs might be worse than earlier ones.

Indeed, so that we do not seem to impose on the shoulders of others onerous and unbearable burdens, while we, saying much and doing nothing or little, are unwilling to move them with our finger, and inasmuch as he who both does and teaches is to be called "great" in the kingdom of Heaven, following the example of Him who undertook to do and teach, and so that we, who, albeit unworthy, function as His vicar on Earth, might set a good example for others, we have decided to aid the Holy Land both personally and through material aid. We have placed with our own hand the emblem of the Cross on our beloved sons Soffredo, cardinal priest of the church of Santa Prassede, and Peter, cardinal deacon of Santa Maria in Vialata, men who are by all means fearers of God, well-known for their learning and honesty, able in both deed and word, whom we favor with a special affection among our other brothers. They are to humbly and devoutly precede the army of the Lord and are to be sustained not by begging for offerings but from our resources and those of our brothers. Through these men we are also arranging to send other suitable aid to that same land. Meanwhile, however, we are dispatching the aforesaid cardinal deacon of Santa Maria in Vialata to the courts of our most beloved sons in Christ, the illustrious kings of France and England, for the purpose of reestablishing peace or, at least, arranging a five-year truce and for the purpose of exhorting the people to the service of the Crucified One. On the other hand, we are sending the aforesaid cardinal priest of Santa Prassede to Venice in search of aid for the Holy Land.

Moreover, by the common advice of our brothers, we have resolved and we strictly command and order you, brother archbishops and bishops and our beloved sons, the abbots, priors, and other prelates of churches, to raise next March a certain number of warriors or, in place of this certain number of warriors, a fixed sum of money (with consideration taken for each person's means), for the purpose of attacking the barbarous tribe of pagans and preserving the Lord's inheritance, which He procured with His own blood. Yet should someone (a thing we cannot believe) presume to oppose such a pious and necessary ordinance, we decree that he is to be punished as a transgressor

against the sacred canons, and we rule that he is to remain suspended from his office until he gives due satisfaction.

Wherefore, trusting in the mercy of God and the authority of the holy Apostles Peter and Paul, we do grant, from that power of binding and loosing that God conferred on us, even though we are unworthy, to all who shall undergo the rigors of this journey in person and at their own expense, full pardon for those sins of theirs for which they have done penance orally and in their hearts, and we promise them the bonus of eternal salvation as the reward of the just. To those, however, who shall not go there in person but who only at their own expense, according to their means and rank, send qualified men there, who are to stay at least two years, and likewise to those who, albeit at the expense of others, still complete in person the rigors of the pilgrimage, which they have undertaken, we grant full pardon for their sins. We also wish people who suitably attend to the relief of this land out of their goods to participate in the remission in relation to the size of their subsidy and especially in proportion to their depth of devotion. In addition, from the time when they have assumed the Cross, we place their possessions under the care of St. Peter and under our own protection—and they are also to stand under the protection of the archbishops and all the prelates of God's Church—ordering that until their death or return is ascertained with full certainty, their possessions remain untouched and stand undisturbed. But if anyone should dare contravene this, he is to be called to account by means of ecclesiastical censure, without appeal. If, indeed, any of those setting out for that place are bound fast by oath to pay interest, you, brother archbishops and bishops, using the same means of coercion, with the obstacle of appeal set aside, are to force their creditors throughout your diocese to absolve them fully from the oath and to desist from further usurious exaction. But if any creditor should force them to pay the interest, using a similar means of coercion, with the obstacle of appeal set aside, you are to compel him to make restitution of it. We order, indeed, Jews to be compelled by you, by our sons the princes, and by secular authority to make restitution of interest to them, and until they remit it to them, we order, under the sanction of excommunication, that every sort of interchange with them, in business as well as in other matters, be refused by all the faithful of Christ.

Let, therefore, no one withhold himself totally from this work, inasmuch as this was not instituted by us but by the apostles themselves who held collections among the gentiles in order to support brethren laboring in Jerusalem. We further do not wish you to lose hope in Divine Mercy, however much the Lord might be irritated by our sins; in fact, He might effect by your hand what He did not grant your forefathers, if (as you ought) you undertake the pilgrimage journey with humility of heart and body. For, perhaps, these forefathers had agreed among themselves and said, "Our own noble hand, and not God, has effected all of this," and they had claimed the glory of victory for themselves and not for God. For we trust that He will not withhold His mercies out of anger—He who, when angered, does not forget to show mercy but admonishes and exhorts us: "Turn to Me and I will turn to you." We also believe that—if you walk in the Law of the Lord and do not follow in the footsteps of those who have become worthless after pursuing that which is worthless, who devoted themselves to the sensuous pleasures of gluttony and drunkenness and did those things in the regions across the sea that they would not have dared do in the lands of their birth without incurring tremendous infamy and considerable disgrace, but, rather, if you place your hope in Him alone, who does not forsake those who hope in Him, and abstain not only from those things that are illicit but even from certain licit actions—He, who cast down the chariot and army of Pharaoh into the sea, will weaken the bow of the mighty and will sweep away the enemies of the Cross from before your eyes, as though they were the filth of the streets. He will give glory not to us or to you but

to His Name—He who is glorious in His saints, wondrous in His majesty, a worker of miracles, and, in the wake of weeping and wailing, the giver of joy and exultation!

Furthermore, so that these commands might be carried out more expeditiously and more perfectly, we have thought it proper to deputize you, our brother archbishop and brother bishops of Nimes and Orange, to preach the Word of the Lord to others and, for the purpose of satisfying this Apostolic mandate, to so motivate your co-bishops and the others who have been invited to the Lord's cause that you might be participants in this remission, and your devotion might shine forth more fully in this endeavor. In order to promote this in an even more praiseworthy fashion, you are to associate yourselves with one of the brothers of the Military Order of the Temple, as well as a second brother of the Order of the Hospital of Jerusalem, men of character and prudence.

Issued at Rieti on the seventeenth day before the Kalends of September.

2. THE LAMBRECHT RITE FOR DEPARTING CRUSADERS

Very few Crusaders read Innocent's letter calling the Crusade. Instead, they internalized the message of the Crusade through recruiting sermons and in the church services that marked their formal joining of the Crusade. Here is an extract from a series of prayers that clerics would offer as they blessed departing Crusaders. It gives a sense of this crucial moment and helps illuminate medieval spirituality. The practice of making a Crusade vow was a deeply religious act, and liturgical sources, such as this German version of the Crusader's departure ritual, are filled with biblical references because they were based on earlier pilgrimage rituals. The purse (sometimes called a scrip) and staff underscore the pilgrim roots of the Crusade itself.

First of all, the Mass of the Holy Cross should be sung, just as it is set forth in the book of the sacraments,[1] and once it has been sung, those who are going to depart ought to prostrate themselves in the shape of the cross, and let them place their clothing and signs [of the cross] near the altar, and let these psalms be sung:

The Lord rules [Ps 22].
May the Lord have mercy [Ps 66].
Sing to the Lord [Pss 95:97; 149].
The Lord has reigned [Ps 96]. Amen.
"Savior of the world, save us whom you redeemed through the cross and [your] blood. We beseech you, our God, to aid us."
Kyrie. Christe. Kyrie.[2] Our Father.[3]

Prayers:

Through the sign of the cross, free us, our God, from our enemies. O Christ, we worship you and bless you, because through your cross you redeemed the world. This sign of the cross will be in heaven when the Lord shall come to judge. O Christ the Savior, save us through the power of [your] cross. You who saved Peter upon the sea, have mercy on us.

Bless, O Lord, this sign of the holy cross that it might be a remedy to save the human race, and vouch through the invocation of your most holy name that those who should take it up or wear it might obtain bodily health and protection for their souls. Through [Christ our Lord, etc.].

Another prayer:

Creator and preserver of the human race, bestower of spiritual grace, granter of eternal

salvation, send forth, O Lord, your spirit over this your creation, so that it [i.e., the spirit] might enable the progress of those who will have partaken of it toward eternal salvation, armed with heavenly defense. Through [Christ our Lord, etc.].

Another prayer:

Lord of Abraham, Lord of Isaac, Lord of Jacob, O Lord who appeared to your servant Moses on Mount Sion, and led forth the sons of Israel from the land of Egypt, assigning to them an angel out of your love [for them], who would guard them by day and by night, we beseech you that you might deign to send your holy angel who might similarly watch over your servants and preserve them from harm from every diabolical attack. Through [Christ our Lord, etc.].

Another prayer:

O Lord, Holy Father, Almighty and Eternal God, you who are leader of the saints and direct the paths of the righteous, direct the angel of peace with your servants, that he might lead them to their determined destinations. May their expedition[4] be agreeable such that no enemy ambushes them upon the way, let the approach of the wicked be far from them, and may the Holy Spirit deign to be present as their marshal. Through the same Lord [etc.].

Then let the signs [of the cross] be sprinkled with holy water and censed and be placed [upon their clothing with these words]:

In the name of the Father and the Son and the Holy Spirit, receive the sign of the cross of Christ both in your hearts and upon your bodies that

---

1. That is, a sacramentary, a liturgical book consulted by the priest or other celebrants.

2. This refers to the liturgical prayer in the Canon of the Mass known as the *Kyrie eleison*, "Lord, have mercy."

3. This refers to the prayer beginning "Our Father," the *Paternoster*, also in the Canon of the Mass.

4. The word here is *comitatus*, which could be translated as "company." It is commonly used in military contexts to designate a military expedition.

you might be preserved from all your enemies and from all the plots of the Devil himself.

Meanwhile, this antiphon should be sung by those standing around them:

O glorious cross, O cross worthy of adoration, O precious wood and wondrous sign through which the Devil is vanquished and the world is redeemed through the blood of Christ.

When this is finished, let the priest say:

[Let us] kneel and pray: Let all the earth worship you, O Lord, and sing to you. Psalm: The Lord is our refuge [Ps 45], etc.
Let us pray: Help, O Lord, we beseech, your servants, that you might heed our prayers during misfortunes and prosperity, and that you might deign to frustrate the impious deeds of our adversaries through the banner of the holy cross, that we might be able to seize the port of salvation. Through [Christ our Lord, etc.].
Lift up [etc.].

Afterward they themselves, if they are able to do so, ought to sing this antiphon:

Sanctify us, O Lord, through the sign of the holy cross, that it might serve as a shield for us against the savage missiles of our enemies. Defend us, O Lord, through the holy wood [of the cross] and through the just price of your blood with which you redeemed us.

Versicle:

We worship you, O Christ, and we bless you. Because through your cross [etc.]. O Lord, our God, save us and also protect with perpetual assistance those whom you caused to rejoice through the holy cross, to his honor. Through [Christ our Lord, etc.].

The blessing for the ship:

O Lord, be appeased by our supplications and send your holy angel from the highest heavens that he might deliver [from harm] this very ship with all sailing in it. Lead it to its intended destinations so that, once it has finished all of its business, you might deign to recall it again in [due] time to its own [home] with every cause for rejoicing. Through [Christ our Lord, etc.].

The blessing upon the wallets and staffs:

O God, come to my aid [Ps 69], in its entirety. Kyrie. Christe. Kyrie. Our Father [etc.]. I believe in God [etc.].[5] Through [Christ our Lord, etc.]. The Lord rules [Ps 22].

Prayers:

Rise up, O Lord God, and let your hand be raised up, lest you forget in the end [cf. Ps 7:7]. Perfect my steps upon your paths, so that my footsteps are not moved [Ps 16:5]. Make wondrous your mercies, you who make safe those trusting in you. May he send us help from the sanctuary and defend us from Sion [Ps 19:3]. Lord, hear my prayer, and my outcry [Ps 101:1].

An oration:

O Lord Jesus Christ, creator and redeemer of the world, you who commanded your blessed apostles to take up staffs when going out for such an important preaching, we earnestly request with humble devotion that you deign to bless these wallets and staffs in such a manner that those who are going to receive them as a token of their pilgrimage and for the sustaining of their

5. This is the Apostles' Creed or another similar creed, from *credo*, "I believe," which is also in the Canon of the Mass.

bodies might receive the fullness of your heavenly favor, so that they might obtain the defense of your blessing, and just as Aaron's staff, by flowering in the temple of the Lord [Nm 17], distinguished itself in its own rank from those of the rebellious Jews, so also these your servants seeking, by this sign, the patronage of the blessed apostles Peter and Paul, you might absolve from all their sins, through which they will be crowned on the day of judgment, freed from the impious, standing on the right side of the Lord.

Another [prayer]:

May the sign of God the Father and the Son and the Holy Spirit descend upon these staffs and upon these wallets which these persons want to carry as a token of their pilgrimage and help those who shall carry them to stand firm, safe and protected from all human and diabolical attacks. Through [Christ our Lord, etc.].

Another [prayer]:

O Lord, you who assemble the scattered and guard those gathered, increase the faith and assurance of your servants, and grant in the future that through the intercession of the blessed Mary, Mother of God, and of the saints N.,[6] whose shrines these individuals desire to visit, and through the intervention of all the saints and of your elect, they might merit to receive the remission of all their sins in this world and the fellowship of all the blessed in the future. Through [Christ our Lord, etc.].

Antiphon:

May the days of repentance come for us, for the redemption of sins, for the salvation of souls.

6. The names (*nomina*) of the saints whose shrines were to be visited were to be inserted here.

Antiphon:

Let us commend ourselves to the power of God in diligent long-suffering through the weapons of righteousness.

Here the staffs are bestowed, while saying:

In the name of our Lord Jesus Christ, take these staffs for sustenance during the journey and the labors of your pilgrimage upon the way, so that you might be able to overcome the troops of your enemies and reach the shrines of the apostles Peter and Paul and other saints to which you desire to hasten, so that, your journey completed, you might deserve to return to us unharmed, preserved by our Lord.

This prayer ought to be said over the wallets:

In the name of our Lord Jesus Christ, receive these wallets as part of the garb[7] of your pilgrimage so that thoroughly emended and cleansed and saved, you might merit to reach the shrines of the apostles Peter and Paul and other saints which you desire to hasten to and so that, your journey accomplished, you might return to us unharmed, that he himself might deign to preserve you, he who when he was rich was made a pauper and destitute for our sake although we were sinners and unworthy, Jesus Christ, our Lord, who with God the Father and the Holy Spirit lives and reigns, God through all the ages.

Prayers:

May the God of our salvation make this journey prosperous for us [Ps 67:20].

7. The word here is *habitum*, the same word used for the monastic habit.

Versicle:

Direct us in the way of peace, O Lord [Ps 143:1].
Through [Christ our Lord, etc.]. Blessed be the
Lord [cf. Lk 1:68–70].

Oration:

Hear us, O Lord our God, and deem worthy to
direct the way of your servants toward the prosper-
ity of your salvation, so that in every occurrence of
worldly vicissitudes, they might be always protected
by your assistance. Through [Christ our Lord, etc.].

Another [prayer]:

O God of endless mercy and boundless majesty
whom neither distance between places nor interval
of time removes from those whom you watch over,
help your servants who trust in you in every place,
and through all the ways in which they will be
traveling, consider them worthy of your being their
leader and companion; so that no adversity may
harm them, no difficulty hinder them, but rather
everything be salutary, everything prosperous for
them, so that under the power of your right hand,
whatever they might strive after with righteous
desire, they might attain with a speedy accom-
plishment. Through [Christ our Lord, etc.].

3. "NOW ONE CAN KNOW AND PROVE," A POEM BY RAIMBAUT DA VAQUEIRAS ON LOYALTY AND THE FOURTH CRUSADE (C. 1203/4)

One of the many troubadours that accompanied the Fourth Crusade, Raimbaut de Vaqueiras was a southern French poet who sang about many of the topics that were important to the knightly lords who were the patrons of his poetry. Trouba-dour songs were sung in camps or in court dining halls, in front of many people, and presented one version of a poem, but they were likely the source of several riffed versions of the same poems. Lords who were able to support several troubadours in their courts were widely considered to be more noble and more chival-rous because they were able to support artists on their largesse. The messages conveyed by troubadours could vary widely, but in many cases Crusade poems played on the dual impacts of a Crusade as a whole: the capturing of mate-rial treasure paralleled the gaining of eternal treasure for pious deeds. This source therefore provides a secular counterpoint to Crusading enterprise described by spiritual sources.

Now one can know and prove
that God to good deeds gives good reward,
and to the valiant marquis he has given gift
   and reward
making his worth stand above the best,
so that the crusaders of France and of Champagne
have asked for him of God as the best of all
to retrieve the sepulchre and the cross
where Jesus was, he who wants in his train
the honoured marquis; and God has given him
   plenty
of good vassals, land and wealth
and of brave heart to do better what behooves him.

He has so much of honour, and wants to keep it,
that he honours God, and worth and generosity
and himself, so that if a thousand barons were
along with him, he would stand over them all
   honour-wise;
he honours himself and honours stranger people
so that he's praised when others are blamed;
he has worn the cross with such honour
that it doesn't seem he lacks other honours,
since with honour he wants to win this world and
   the other
and God has given him strength, wit and learning
to have them both, and he endeavours at his best.

He who made air and sky and earth and sea
and cold and heat and rain and wind and thunder

wants all good men to cross the sea under his
    guidance
lead as he lead Melchior and Caspar [i.e., two of the
    three biblical "Wise Men"]
to Bethlehem, since plains and mountains
part us from the Turks and God won't utter a word.
It befits us, for whom he was set onto a cross,
to cross thereto; and he who stays here
wants to see an ill life and a grievous death:
because we linger in filthy sin, that man must
    dread,
and from which each'll be delivered by bathing in
    the Jordan.

God let himself be sold to save us,
and suffered death and endured his passion;
fiendish Jews insulted him for our sake,
and he was beaten and bound to a stake,
and raised onto the beam that stood in the mud
and he was lashed with knotted scourges
and crowned with thorns on the cross:
so, hard-hearted is the man that doesn't mourn the
    harm
the Turks cause us, in wanting to keep
the lands where God wanted to dwell, alive and
    dead:
so we ought to wage war and stir huge fights.

But our sin thwarts us to such a degree
that we live like dead men, I can't tell how,
since there is no man so brave nor so valiant that,
if he has joy somewhere, he shan't have sorrows
    somewhere else,
nor is there honour that doesn't turn to shame:
the luckiest has one pleasure out of a thousand
    grievances.
But God, in whose name one crosses himself, is joy,
so that he who gains of Him can't lose;
so I love better, if He so likes,
to die there than to stay alive here
in peril, were Germany mine.

St. Nicholas of Bari lead our fleet
and those of Champagne lift their banner

cry the marquis "Monferrat and the lion!"
and the Flemish count cry "Flanders" while
    strongly slashing;
and let each wound with his sword and break his
    lance,
so that, soon, we'll have the Turks all dead and
    routed
and we'll win on the field the true cross
we have lost; and let the brave kings
    of Spain
make great armies triumph over the Moors,
since the marquis attacks and besieges
the sultan, and will presently cross to Rumania
    [i.e., Turkey].

Our Lord commands and advises us all
to go retrieve the sepulchre and cross;
and he who wants to be of his train,
let him die for Him if he wants to stay alive
in Heaven, and let him do what he can
to cross the sea and kill those curs.

Fair Knight for whom I write songs and lyrics
    [note that this is a reference to his lover, not
    his lord],
I don't know whether to renounce for your sake, or
    wear the cross
nor how to go, nor how to remain;
so much your beautiful body pleases me,
that I die if I see you and if can't see you:
I fear to die, in anyone's company but yours.

4. GRATIAN'S *DECRETUM* ON THE RULES OF WAR

The most important medieval legal text is
Gratian's *Decretum*. Gratian was the name given
to the author of a work of canon, or church, law.
Recent scholarship has determined that the
Decretum is actually the work of several scholars
on at least two different versions (like a modern
textbook, whose second edition may involve
new authors). The first version was the work of
an Italian bishop and lawyer named Gratian
who worked around 1140–50, taught at the

famous law school of Bologna, and eventually became bishop of Chiusi. The *Decretum* is a handbook for church lawyers to help them debate important arguments. The second part presents complex example cases to demonstrate the ways legal issues should be resolved. It is divided into cases about general topics, which are then subdivided into several different questions on specific topics. In each question, Gratian sets out his argument, using quotations from the Bible, previous popes, and early church councils. Alongside the quotes, he makes legal pronouncements in each section, which he calls canons—hence the name "canon law." Because of the enormous length of the text and its many detailed examples, we have highlighted only a few excerpts here, but some translated sections of Gratian's work are available in other sources, included in the "Further Reading" section below. (These selections were initially used in the game book for a Reacting to the Past game on the Second Crusade written by Helen Gaudette.)

Question I

Gratian: It would seem that it is contrary to the teaching of the Gospel to serve as a soldier, since the point of all soldiering is either to resist injury or to carry out vengeance; but injury is either warded off from one's own person or from one's associates, both of which are prohibited by the law of the Gospel. For it is said: "If anyone strikes you on the right cheek, turn to him the other also" (Matthew 5:39); and again: "If anyone forces you to go one mile, go with him two miles" (Matthew 5:41); likewise, the Apostle said to the Romans: "Beloved, never avenge yourselves, but leave it to the wrath of God" (Matthew 12:19). What else, then, is meant by these passages, except that we are barred from resisting injury?

1. Furthermore, when Peter defended his master with a sword, Christ said: "Put your sword into its sheath"; "Do you think that I

cannot appeal to my Father, and he will send me more than twelve legions of angels?" (Matthew 26:52). Finally, as is read about St. Andrew, when there was a rush of people to rescue him from the clutches of a wicked judge and to save him from an unjust death, he urged upon them patience, both in word and deed, lest they prevent his martyrdom. What else are we hereby incited to do than patiently to endure similar trials?

2. Next it is said in Proverbs: "Vengeance is mine, and I will repay, says the Lord." [The passage is actually Deuteronomy 32:35.] Likewise, it is said in the Gospel: "Judge not, and you will not be judged" (Mathew 7:11). . . . What else is enjoined by all this if not that punishment of delinquents is to be reserved to divine judgment?

Since, therefore, as was stated above, all soldiering seems to aim at resisting an attack or at inflicting vengeance, and since each of these is prohibited by the law of the Gospel, it appears that it is a sin to serve as a soldier. . . .

Gratian: Here is how we answer these arguments:

The precepts of patience have to prevail less in outward deed than in the preparation of the heart.

Hence Augustine said in his *Sermon on the Child of the Centurion*:

Canon 2. The precepts of patience have to be observed through firmness of the mind, not in outward attitude

The just and pious man ought to be ready to put up with the malice of those he wants to become good, in order that the number of the good may increase, instead of adding himself by equal malice to the number of the wicked. In sum, these precepts are rather for the preparation of the heart which is internal, than for the deed which is in the open; so that patience and benevolence are to be confined to the secret of the mind, while what has to show in the open would seem to profit those we want to become better. . . .

Likewise, Augustine to Boniface:

Canon 3. Many can please God in the profession of arms

Do not think that none can please God while serving in arms. . . . Therefore keep this in mind first of all, when you prepare to fight, that your valor, including your bodily courage, is a gift of God. Thus you will care not to use a gift of God against the Lord. For, when it has been vowed, faith is not to be kept even toward the enemy against whom war is being waged; how much more toward a friend whom one is fighting for? To strive for peace is a matter of willing, but war should be of necessity, so that God may free us from necessity and conserve us in peace. For peace is not pursued in order to wage war, but war is waged in order to gain peace. Be therefore peaceable while you wage war, so that you may in winning lead over to the benefit of peace those whom you defeat. . . . It is therefore necessity, not will, that crushes the fighting enemy. Just as he who fights and resists is checked by violence, mercy is due to the vanquished, to the captive, mostly when no trouble to the peace is to be feared on his part.

Likewise, Augustine *Against the Manichaeans*:

Canon 4. What is rightfully to be blamed in war

What is to be blamed in war? Is it the death of some who are to die in any case, so that others may be forced to peaceful subjection? To reprove this is cowardice, not religion. What is rightly reproved in war are love of mischief, revengeful cruelty, fierce implacable enmity, wild resistance, lust of power, and such like. And it is generally to punish these things, when force is required to inflict punishment, that, in obedience to God or some lawful authority, good men undertake wars, when they find themselves in such a position as regards the conduct of human affairs, that this very position justly compels them either to give such orders or to obey them. Thus John does not order soldiers to lay

down their arms, and Christ urges that money be given to Caesar, because soldiers need to get their pay on account of war. For this natural order which seeks the peace of mankind ordains that the authority and resolve to undertake war lie with the princes.

1. But if war is undertaken to serve human greed, this does not trouble the saints, over whom no one can have any power but what is given from above. For there is no power but from God, who either orders or permits. Thus a righteous man, who happens to be serving even under a sacrilegious king, can rightfully engage in combat at his command if, keeping up the order instead of peace, it is either certain that what he is ordered is not contrary to God's law, or it is not certain whether it is contrary to God's law. . . .

Gratian: From all this we gather that soldiering is not a sin, and that the precepts of patience are to be observed in the preparation of the heart, not in the ostentation of the body.

Question II

Gratian: Now, as to what constitutes a just war, Isidore in *Twenty Books of Etymologies* says:

Canon 1. What is a just war

That war is just which is waged by an edict in order to regain what has been stolen or to repel the attack of enemies. A judge is called such because he pronounces justice to the people, or because he adjudicates justly. To adjudicate justly is to judge justly. For he is no judge who has no justice within himself.

Likewise, Augustine in *Seven Questions concerning the Heptateuch* says:

Canon 2. It is of no concern to justice whether one fights openly or by ambushes

Our Lord God himself gave the order to Joshua to set up an ambush behind him, that is, to arrange his warriors so as to trap the enemy in an ambush. This teaches us that such things are not done unjustly by those who fight a just war; so that the just man doesn't need particularly to worry about this, except that war be undertaken by one who has the right to do so. For this right does not belong to everyone. Yet when a just war is undertaken, it does not affect justice whether one fights openly or by ambushes. Just wars are usually defined as those which have for their end the avenging of injuries, when it is necessary by war to constrain a nation or a city which has either neglected to punish an evil action committed by its citizens, or to restore what has been taken unjustly. But also this kind of war is certainly just which is ordered by God, who knows what is owed to everyone; in which case the leader of the army or the people itself are not to be deemed authors but agents of the war.

Gratian: Since therefore the just war is one which is waged by an edict, or by which injustices arc avenged, it is asked how the children of Israel fought just wars.

On this subject, Augustine wrote in his *Questions on [the book of] Numbers* that:

Canon 3. The sons of Israel were refused passage, and therefore they waged just wars

One ought indeed to note how just wars were waged by the sons of Israel against the Amorites. For they were denied innocent passage, which ought to have been granted according to the most equitable law governing human society.

Question III

Gratian: But injury done to associates should not be repelled, as shown by examples and authorities. . . . Thus we also read about the faithful that they suffered with joy to be robbed of their goods, without asking for any assistance by others; rather, they rejoiced at being found worthy of bearing disgrace in the name of Christ.

And the Apostle [Paul] also advises the Corinthians, in his first epistle to them, patiently to put up with injury and fraud, rather than to scandalize their brethren by asserting their rights. . . . Since therefore he who is being protected from injury by the force of arms is no less scandalized than he whose stolen property is being claimed before a judge, it is evident that armed assistance ought not to be requested. And what ought not to be requested, ought not to be granted in law. But on the other hand, many things are being regularly granted that are not legally claimed. The virtuous will indeed not regularly claim that an injury be sanctioned, lest he render all evil for an evil; and yet the judge would rightly inflict such punishment; nor would he do it if he did not thereby render a good deed for an evil one. . . .

Likewise, Ambrose writes in the first book of his work *On the Duties of Ministers*:

Canon 5. He is full of justice who protects his country from barbarians

The courage that protects one's country from barbarians in war, or defends the weak in peace, or associates against brigands, is full of justice.

Likewise, Ambrose writes in the first book of his work *On the Duties of Ministers*:

Canon 7. He who does not ward off an injury from an associate is similar to him who caused it

The law of valor lies not in inflicting injury but in repelling it; for he who fails to ward off an injury from an associate if he can do so is quite as blamable as he who inflicts it. It is here, therefore, that Moses the saint gave the first proofs of his courage at war. For when he saw a Hebrew being mistreated by an Egyptian, he defended him by striking the Egyptian and hiding him in the sand. Solomon too said: Deliver him who is being led to death (Proverbs 24:11).

Question IV

Gratian: Likewise, this Gospel sentence, "He who resorts to the sword shall perish by the sword," that is advanced as an objection, is explained by

Augustine in Book II Chap. 70 of his *Against the Manichaeans*:

Canon 36. Who should be said to resort to the sword

He resorts to the sword who has armed himself to spill the blood of another without the order or assent of a legitimate power.

Gratian: It has been briefly shown that the good laudably pursue the wicked, and that the wicked damnably pursue the good. . . . It has been shown that vengeance may be exerted. It now remains to show who is to exert it and by what means, and that those who are punished are more cherished than those who remain unpunished: both points are proven with many authorities.

Likewise, Augustine writes in *On the Lord's Sermon on the Mountain*:

Canon 51. Vengeance that aims at correction is not to be prohibited

That vengeance which aims at correction is not prohibited; it even belongs to mercy, and it is not in conflict with the attitude whereby he who wants someone to be punished is ready to suffer more from him; but only he is apt to inflict this vengeance who has overcome by the mildness of love that hatred which usually impels those who avenge themselves. Indeed, it is not to be feared that the parents would hate their little son when he is being chidden in order not to sin again. . . . No one should therefore exert vengeance but he on whom regular power has been conferred thereto, and who punishes like a father striking his little child, unable as he is to hate him owing to his age. . . .

Gratian: From all this we gather that vengeance is to be inflicted not out of passion for vengeance itself, but out of zeal for justice; nor in order that hatred be vented, but that evil deeds be corrected. But since retribution is sometimes inflicted by destroying goods, sometimes by flogging, sometimes even by death, we ask whether it is sinful for the judge or his minister to put the guilty to death.

Question V

Gratian: Now, that nobody is allowed to kill anyone is proved by that precept whereby the Lord in the Decalogue prohibited homicide, saying: "Thou shalt not kill." Likewise, it is said in the Gospel that "Whoever takes the sword, shall perish by the sword."

Likewise, it is said by Pope Gregory:

Canon 7. Those who are accused of shedding blood must be defended by the Church

Let the Church defend those who are accused of bloodshed, lest it partake in the spilling of blood.

Gratian: Hence it appears that the wicked are to be corrected by flogging, not to be quelled by maiming or temporal death. But an objection arises from what the Lord said to Moses: "Do not suffer evildoers to live" (Exodus 22:18). . . . This precept forbids thus anyone to arm himself by his own authority to inflict death on somebody; it does not forbid putting the culprits to death by the command of the law. For he who in the exercise of public power puts to death the wicked by the command of the law is neither considered a transgressor of this precept nor a stranger to the heavenly fatherland.

Therefore Augustine wrote to Publicola:

Canon 8. It is no sin to kill a man in the exercise of a public function

As to putting men to death in order that nobody be killed by them, I do not approve of it, except perhaps by a soldier or by someone held thereto owing to a public function, so that he does not do it for himself but for others, or for the city where he finds himself, having been conferred legitimate power in conformity with his person. As to those who are held back by some terror from doing evil, they may themselves draw some benefit from it. Hence it is said: We should not resist evil, lest you take delight in vengeance, which feeds the mind in others' misfortune; yet we should not for all that neglect the correction of evil men. . . .

Likewise Augustine, *On Free Will*, Book 1:

Canon 41. He does not sin who kills a criminal by virtue of his functions

If killing a man is indeed homicide, it sometimes can happen without sin. For neither a soldier killing an enemy, nor a judge or his minister killing a criminal, nor someone inadvertently or imprudently throwing a spear would sin, in my opinion, when they killed a man. Nor are they usually called homicides.

The same, in *Questions on Leviticus*:

When a man is justly killed, it is the law, not you, who kills him.

Likewise, Pope Nicholas to the army of the Franks:

Canon 46. Whoever dies in the fight against the infidel is deserving of the celestial kingdom

We want all of you to know charity, since none of those who will have faithfully died in this battle (we say this without wishing it) shall in the least be denied the celestial kingdom.

Likewise, Augustine to Boniface:

For who of us would have someone of his enemies, I say not die, but even lose something? But if the house of David could not regain peace otherwise than by the death of Absalom, his son, in the war he was waging against the father—although the latter had been at great pains to enjoin his men as far as possible to take him safe and alive so that he might repent and obtain his pardon from paternal affection—what else remained than to weep his loss and to soothe his sorrow at the thought of peace being restored in his kingdom?

Gratian: If therefore saintly men and public powers waging war did not transgress that command, "Thou shalt not kill," while inflicting death on all villains deserving it; if the soldier, acting in obedience to his authorities, is not guilty of homicide when, following their order, he kills any villain; if killing murderers and punishing poisoners does not amount to spilling blood but to serving the law; if the peace of the church allays the sorrow caused by the lost ones; if those who, inflamed by the zeal of their Catholic mother, put to death the excommunicated are not considered homicides—then it is obvious that it is allowed not only to whip but also to kill the wicked.

5. INNOCENT III CRITICIZES THE CRUSADE AFTER THE ATTACK ON ZARA (DECEMBER 1202)

Crusades were not immune to the effects of Murphy's Law, and necessity made strange decisions seem more palatable. The attack on Zara was pitched as one of necessity to the rank-and-file Crusader—the Crusade's debt to Venice was so substantial, the need for supplies so considerable, and the betrayal of Zara so tragic—but Pope Innocent III did not see it in that light. This letter leaves no doubt that Innocent was enraged by the conquest of Zara but that he also saw it as a teachable moment, a chance to remind the Crusaders that they had sworn a vow focused on the recapture of Jerusalem but had been distracted by the worldly complications of Venice's territorial ambitions. For a pope who had worked so hard to bring the goals of the church in alignment with the material necessities of a Crusade, the attack on Zara seemed to be a betrayal of the earlier collaboration that had defined the early part of the Fourth Crusade.

To the counts, barons, and all the Crusaders *without* greeting:

We sorrow not a little and we are disturbed that in those instances in which we have been accustomed to grant the grace of remission and to offer the promise of an increase in eternal recompense, now (and we do not say this without a good deal of grief) we are compelled to deny the consolation of our salutation and the protection of an Apostolic blessing. For behold, your gold has turned to base metal and your silver has almost completely rusted since, departing from the purity of your plan and turning aside from the path onto the impassable road, you have, so to speak, withdrawn your hand from the plow and looked backward with Lot's wife. For when, as you were fleeing Egypt, you should have hastened to the land flowing with honey and milk, you turned away, going astray in the direction of the desert. There you recalled to mind how in Egypt you sat amidst the fleshpots, and you hungered not only for garlic and melons, but you thirsted after the blood of your brothers. We are mindful, indeed, of the serpent of old; how God established enmity between the seed of the woman and its offspring following the fall of the first human. Because it was ineffective against the head, it lay in ambush for the heel. It hid itself along the path so that it might at least strike horses' hooves and might bring down the rider along with the horse, seeing to it (by virtue of the usual craft of deceit and the malice of accustomed evil) that insofar as you offended in one matter, you destroyed the merit of your entire labor—even as a trifle of leaven spoils an entire mass and they who are guilty of one action [against the Law] are guilty of all. Inasmuch as that ancient enemy, who is the Devil and Satan, the seducer of the whole world, is mindful of the fact that no one has greater love than one who lays down his life for his friends, in order to deprive you of the reward and good will for such love, he caused you to make war against your brothers and to unfurl your battle standards initially against people of the Faith, so that you might pay him the first fruits of your pilgrimage and pour out for demons both your own and your brothers' blood. Having the appearance of going not to Jerusalem but rather of descending into Egypt, you went down into Jericho on your way from Jerusalem and consequently fell in among thieves. Although they stripped from you the mantle of virtues and laid on you, once you were despoiled, the blows of sins, nevertheless, so far they have not wished to depart or to leave you half alive, because up to now afflictions are visited upon you by evil angels, with the result that, just as you turn aside to the islands for your necessities and turn spoils taken from Christians into your own income, so also (we learned) you recently did the same at Zara.

For when you arrived there by ship, after first unfurling your battle standards in challenge to the city, you set up tents for a siege. You surrounded the city on every side with trenches and undermined its walls, not without a good deal of bloodletting. Whenever the citizens wished to submit, along with the Venetians, to your judgment (and not even in this could they find any mercy in you), they hung images of the Cross around the walls. But you attacked the city and the citizens to the not insubstantial injury of the Crucified One, and what is more, by violent skill you compelled them to surrender. Yet, reverence for the Cross you took up, or devotion to our most beloved son in Christ, Emeric, distinguished king of the Hungarians, and to that nobleman, Duke Andrew, his brother, who have assumed the sign of the Cross for the aid of the Holy Land, or, at least, the authority of the Apostolic See, which took care to prohibit you strictly from attempting to invade or violate the lands of Christians unless either they wickedly impede your journey or another just or necessary cause should, perhaps, arise that would allow you to act otherwise in accordance with the guidance offered by our legate, should have deterred you from such a very wicked plan.

Lest, indeed, the foregoing prohibition be heard with little zeal, should there be those who presumed to contravene it, we ruled they would be bound by the chain of excommunication and denied the benefit of the indulgence that the Apostolic See granted to the crusaders. In other respects, although our beloved son Peter, cardinal priest of the church of San Marcello, legate of the Apostolic See, had taken care to explain to some of you the meaning of our prohibition and, finally, our letter was publicly presented to you, you submitted to neither God nor the Apostolic See but compelled the pitiable Zarans to surrender. The Venetians, therefore, knocked down the walls of this same city in your sight, they despoiled churches, they destroyed buildings, and you shared the spoils of Zara with them.

Lest, therefore, you add sin to sin and there be fulfilled in you, as it is written, "The sinner values little when he has arrived in the depths of vice," we admonish all of you and exhort you more intently, and we command you through this Apostolic letter, and we strictly order under the threat of anathema" that you neither destroy Zara any more than it has been destroyed up to this point nor cause it to be destroyed (or permit it, insofar as it is in your power). Rather arrange to restore to the envoys of that same king all that has been taken. Moreover, you should realize that you lie under the sentence of excommunication and cannot share in the grant of remission promised you.

Issued at the Lateran.

Section Two
"Feudalism" and Pronoia

The second section covers the institution that (until quite recently) was collectively called "feudalism." Although modern historians have since rejected the notion of such a unified, culturally cohesive concept, scholars do still emphasize the importance of several main themes within feudal society—a more loosely defined term that suggests similarities but not underlying structures. Key to the feudal society of contemporary Christian Europe were notions of loyalty—expressed through public oaths—and military service as a part of a land-tenure system. These allegiances created an intimate bond of honor between men of similar social standing, but they also reinforced a complex shame- and guilt-based system that punished those who failed to uphold their oaths and ride to war when necessary. The rituals of loyalty were meant to cement the connections between lords and vassals, and they often involved relics and religious symbolism to make clear that, while the feudal society was organized by men, it was protected and ordained by God. Fundamentally, it was the enterprise of the material sword, although guaranteed and supported by the spiritual sword. In addition to these elements, ritual played an important part, both in the decision to ride to war and in creating new or expanded bonds within the class of aristocratic males, both lay and religious, who comprised the leadership of both the military and religious spheres. Additionally, this section contains one of the precious few descriptions of Byzantine *pronoia*, the variation on feudal society that was the prevailing set of social norms in contemporary Byzantium. While a strict caesaropapism made the debate about the distinctions between the spiritual and the material swords moot in the Byzantine Empire, the implications of good organization in the empire were still important to the church because of the emperor's dual mandate of protecting both the church itself and the empire's people.

1. HOMAGE AND FEALTY TO THE COUNT OF FLANDERS (1127)

Oaths of loyalty were at the heart of the feudal society of the High Middle Ages. This example—of an oath sworn to the new Count William of Flanders after the death of the previous count, Charles, dated to 1127—presents the key elements of the vassal's obligations to his lord. The provision that the vassal receive lands—from which he would draw an income and could support his military vocation—from the lord was part of the exchange, and the oath of loyalty from the vassal was a promise that, when the lord needed military support for a war or for the collection of taxes, the vassal would serve dutifully. Notice here the role that relics, the remains of saints, play as talismans of power that guarantee—in the important third (referencing the Trinity) vow—the oaths sworn.

Through the whole remaining part of the day, those who had been previously enfeoffed by the most pious count Charles, did homage to the count, taking up now again their fiefs and offices and whatever they had before rightfully and legitimately obtained. On Thursday the seventh of April, homages were again made to the count being completed in the following order of faith and security.

First they did their homage thus, the count asked if he was willing to become completely his man, and the other replied, "I am willing"; and with clasped hands, surrounded by the hands of the count, they were bound together by a kiss. Secondly, he who had done homage gave his fealty to the representative of the count in these words, "I promise on my faith that I will in future be faithful to count William, and will observe my homage to him completely against all persons in good faith and without deceit." Thirdly, he took his oath to this upon the relics of the saints. Afterward, with a little rod which the count held in his hand, he gave investitures to all who by this agreement had given their security and homage and accompanying oath.

2. THE FUNCTION OF KNIGHTHOOD BY JOHN OF SALISBURY (C. 1159)

Knightly values were recognized in the practical iterations of the oath sworn by the vassals to their lords, but these same values were also examined in the theoretical treatises of the leading European intellectuals. John of Salisbury was the bishop of Chartres and an eminent philosopher and theologian. Here, he meditates on the value of the knightly class to the religious order of the Latin Christian world and the way in which knights could and should contribute to the important religious and social work that was performed by the church.

But what is the office of the duly ordained soldiery? To defend the Church, to assail infidelity, to venerate the priesthood, to protect the poor from injuries, to pacify the province, to pour out their blood for their brothers (as the formula of their oath instructs them), and, if need be, to lay down their lives. The high praises of God are in their throat, and two-edged swords are in their hands to execute punishment on the nations and rebuke upon the peoples, and to bind their kings in chains and their nobles in links of iron. But to what end? To the end that they may serve madness, vanity, avarice, or their own private self-will? By no means.

Rather to the end that they may execute the judgment that is committed to them to execute; wherein each follows not his own will but the deliberate decision of God, the angels, and men, in accordance with equity and the public utility. . . . For soldiers that do these things are "saints," and are the more loyal to their prince in proportion as they more zealously keep the faith of God; and they advance the more successfully the honour of their own valour as they seek the more faithfully in all things the glory of their God.

3. THE CHIVALRIC IDEAL BY DÍAZ DE GÁMEZ (C. 1402, BASED ON EARLIER MODELS)

Gutierre Díaz de Gámez was a Castilian knight who served widely in the armies of King Pedro III of Castile and who wrote about his contemporary world. Although this text dates to the century after the Fourth Crusade, it presents one of the clearest crystallizations of how knights understood their place in the social order of the Late Middle Ages. Díaz de Gámez presents a number of important virtues that describe knighthood as an honorable and worthy station in life for its own sake, rather than for serving some ulterior purpose. It presents, then, a kind of contrasting ideal to that offered by John of Salisbury, although they agree on many of the virtues required of good secular lords.

Now is it fitting that I should tell what it is to be a knight: whence comes this name of knight; what manner of a man a knight should be to have a right to be called a knight; and what profit the good knight is to the country wherein he lives. I tell you that men call knight the man who, of custom, rides upon a horse. He who, of custom, rides upon another mount, is no knight; but he who rides upon a horse is not for that reason a knight; he only is rightly called a knight who makes it his calling. Knights have not been chosen to ride an ass or a mule; they have not been taken from among feeble or timid or cowardly souls, but from among men who are strong and full of energy, bold and without fear; and for this reason there is no other beast that so befits a knight as a good horse. Thus have horses been found that in the thick of battle have shown themselves as loyal to their masters as if they had been men. There are horses who are so strong, fiery, swift, and faithful, that a brave man, mounted on a good horse, may do more in an hour of fighting than ten or maybe a hundred could have done afoot. For this reason do men rightly call him knight.

What is required of a good knight? That he should be noble. What means noble and nobility? That the heart should be governed by the virtues. By what virtues? By the four that I have already named. These four virtues are sisters and so bound up one with the other, that he who has one, has all, and he who lacks one, lacks the others also. So the virtuous knight should be wary and prudent, just in the doing of justice, continent and temperate, enduring and courageous; and with all he must have great faith in God, hope at HIS glory, that he may attain the reward for the good that he has done, and finally he must have charity and the love of his neighbour.

Of what profit is a good knight? I tell you that through good knights is the king and the kingdom honoured, protected, feared, and defended. I tell you that the king, when he sends forth a good knight with an army and entrusts him with a great enterprise, on sea or on land, has in him a pledge of victory. I tell you that without good knights, the king is like a man who has neither feet nor hands.

4. THE CORONATION (1189) OF KING RICHARD THE LIONHEART BY ROGER OF HOWDEN (C. 1200)

The rituals that invested rulers with their office were highly orchestrated. Since leaders understood themselves as "serving by the grace of God," coronations were deeply religious affairs, and ecclesiastical officials often took great pains to ensure that the secular rulers being crowned were reminded of the theoretical supremacy that religious power had over the physical world. The metaphor of the two swords (laid out by Pope Gelasius, above) was a powerful indicator of the ways that the world was separated into physical or temporal power and spiritual or religious power.

First came the bishops, abbots, and large numbers of the clergy, wearing silken hoods, preceded by the cross, taper-bearers, censers, and holy water, as far as the door of the king's inner chamber; where they received the before-named duke [i.e., Richard the Lionheart—who was duke of Aquitaine before his coronation] and escorted him to the church of Westminster, as far as the high altar, in solemn procession, with chants of praise, while all the way along which they went, from the door of the king's chamber to the altar, was covered with woolen cloth. The order of the procession was as follows: First came the clergy in their robes, carrying holy water, and the cross, tapers, and censers. Next came the priors, then the abbots, and then the bishops, in the midst of whom walked four barons, bearing four candlesticks of gold; after whom came Godfrey de Lucy, bearing the king's cap [of maintenance], and John Marshal by him, carrying two great and massive spurs of gold. After these came William Marshal, earl of Striguil, bearing the royal sceptre of gold, on the top of which was a cross of gold, and by him William Fitz-Patrick, earl of Salisbury, bearing a rod of gold, having on its top a dove of gold. After them came David, earl of Huntingdon, brother of the king of Scotland, John, earl of Mortaigne, the duke's brother, and Robert, earl of Leicester, carrying three golden swords from the king's treasury, the scabbards of which were worked all over with gold; the earl of Mortaigne walking in the middle. Next came six earls and six barons, carrying on their shoulders a very large chequer, upon which were placed the royal arms and robes; and after them William de Mandeville, earl of Aumarle, carrying a great and massive crown of gold, decorated on every side with precious stones. Next came Richard, duke of Normandy, Hugh, bishop of Durham, walking at his right hand, and Reginald, bishop of Bath, at his left, and four barons holding over them a canopy of silk on four lofty spears. Then followed a great number of earls, barons, knights, and others, both clergy and laity, as far as the porch of the church, and dressed in their robes, entered with the duke, and proceeded as far as the choir.

When the duke had come to the altar, in presence of the archbishops, bishops, clergy, and people, kneeling before the altar, with the holy Evangelists placed before him, and many relics of the saints, according to custom, he swore that he would all the days of his life observe peace, honor, and reverence towards God, the Holy Church, and its ordinances. He also swore that he would exercise true justice and equity towards the people committed to his charge. He also swore that he would abrogate bad laws and unjust customs, if any such had been introduced into his kingdom, and would enact good laws, and observe the same without fraud or evil intent. After this they took off all his clothes from the waist upwards, except his shirt and breeches; his shirt having been previously separated over the shoulders; after which they shod him with sandals embroidered with gold. Then Baldwin, archbishop of Canterbury, pouring holy oil upon his head, anointed him king in three places, on his head, breast, and arms, which signifies glory, valour, and knowledge, with suitable prayers for the occasion; after which the said archbishop placed a consecrated linen cloth on his head, and upon that the cap which Geoffrey de Lucy had carried. They then clothed him in the royal robes, first a tunic, and then a dalmatic; after which the said archbishop delivered to him the sword of rule, with which to crush evildoers against the Church: this done, two earls placed the spurs upon his feet, which John Marshal had carried. After this being robed in a mantle, he was led to the altar, where the said archbishop forbade him, in the name of Almighty God, to presume to take upon him this dignity, unless he had the full intention inviolably to observe the oaths and vows before mentioned which he had made; to which he made answer that, with God's assistance, he would without reservation observe them all. After this, he himself took the crown from the altar and gave it to the archbishop; on which, the archbishop delivered it to him, and placed it upon his head, it being supported by two earls in consequence of its extreme weight. After this, the archbishop delivered to him the sceptre to hold in his right hand, while he held the rod of royalty in his left; and, having been thus crowned, the king was led back to his seat by the before-named bishops of Durham and Bath, preceded by the taper-bearers and the three swords before-mentioned. After this, the mass of our Lord was commenced, and, when they came to the offertory, the before-named bishops led him to the altar, where he offered one mark of the purest gold, such being the proper offering for the king at each coronation; after which, the bishops before-named led him back to his seat. The mass having been concluded, and all things solemnly performed, the two bishops before-named, one on the right hand the other on the left, led him back from the church to his chamber, crowned, and carrying a sceptre in his right hand and the rod of royalty in his left, the procession going in the same order as before. Then the procession returned to the choir, and our lord the king put off his royal crown and robes of royalty, and put on a crown and robes that were lighter; and, thus crowned, went to dine; on which the archbishops and bishops took their seats with him at the table, each according to his rank and dignity. The earls and barons also served in the king's palace, according to their several dignities; while the citizens of London served in the cellars, and the citizens of Winchester in the kitchen.

5. A GRANT OF PRONOIA TO MICHAEL SAVENTZES (1321)

Pronoia was the Byzantine parallel to the feudal organization of Western Europe. In many ways, it resembled the feudal obligations of the lords and vassals whose relationships were memorialized above. The Byzantine system, however, gave titles that were not usually inherited by generations, were appointed by the emperor or his subordinates, and were rendered for revenues and goods instead of in explicit military services. While it was often presented as being meritocratic to contemporaries, the class of people to whom pronoia allotments were granted were still wealthier and capable of extracting a series of revenues that were owed to the imperial treasurer.

Since we have been ordered by our mighty and holy lord and emperor to make an assessor's equalization and reestablishment in the theme of the God-saved city of Thessaloniki, that is, of the properties of the archons of the kin of our mighty and holy lord and emperor and of the other archons—ecclesiastic, monastic, military, of archons, *chrysoboullata*—and the rest, and to confer upon each his proper quantity, finding among other [things] the *oikonomia* held by *kyr* (a Byzantine version of the Western "Sir") Michael Saventzes of the Thessalonian mega allagion, we confer this upon him from the mercy of our mighty and holy lord and emperor toward us, which has the following:

In the katepanikion of Akros [i.e., Longos] in the village of Psalis: Nicholas Photenos has a wife Anna, sons Demetrios, Athanasios, and Lampetes, a daughter [vacant], a brother John, 1 ass, 100 goats, a vineyard in two parcels by purchase from Philippopolites of 12/3 modioi, and 30 modioi of land. 3 nomismata. Michael, the son of Stamates Vardas, has a wife [vacant], a vineyard of 12/3 modioi, and 50 modioi of land. 11/3 nomismata.

In the same village from the oikonomia of Smyrnaios: Gregory, the son of Michael Vechas, has a brother Nicholas, a sister-in-law by him Argyre, a son John, 30 goats, a vineyard of 1 modios, and 40 modioi of land. 11/2 nomismata. In the village of Phournia: Demetrios, the son of Modestos Tzykalas, has a wife Kale, sons Stamates and George, a daughter [vacant], 1 ox, 2 cows, 3 beehives, a vineyard of 1 modios. 1 nomisma. In the village of Ourliakon from the oikonomia of the reverend monastery of Akapniou: Demetrios, the son-in-law of George Pissyris, that is, Kometzianos, has a wife Kale, a son Michael, 1 ox, 2 cows, a garden of 2 modioi in which there are 2 pear trees. . . .

Altogether, these [are] 35 nomismata, so as to make the whole 70 nomismata, which

[Saventzes] ought to hold and enjoy and to take for himself the income from them, and to demand the oikoumenon through two payments yearly, that is, half in September and the other half in March, and to receive for the oikomodion 1 modios of grain for each 3 hyperpyra [of telos], for the oinometrion 1 measure of local wine per 1 hyperpyron [of telos], corvees for 12 days per year, as the paroikos is able, and the customary three kaniskia per year. For this our present praktikon is signed as customary and guaranteed by a lead seal, which is given to the distinguished kyr Michael Saventzes in surety in the month of February, indiction 4.

[signed] -I- The servants of our mighty and holy lord and emperor, the assessors of the theme of Thessaloniki, sevastoi Constantine Pergamenos and George Pharisaios +

Section Three

The Venetian Republic

This section describes the history of the Venetian Republic, one of the four factions in this Reacting to the Past game, but one of the most infrequently discussed great powers in medieval Europe. There are three texts here, but they are only a small sample of the total available material from Venice. The first text is a description— literally titled as a "praise"—of the city of Venice by the historian Marino Sanudo, who travelled widely but was a native of the Venetian Republic. These texts help fill out the picture of what the city of Venice was like and provide a foundation for Venetian characters and their partners. The second text is the famous Chrysobull (gold-sealed letter) of 1082, which granted expansive and lasting privileges to the Venetians in the city of Constantinople and helped cement their hold on a major share of the commerce of the Byzantine Empire. The third text is part of a history of Venice written by Martino da Canale (c. 1270) that includes both the city's origins and an account of recent interactions between Venice, the Crusading movements of the twelfth century, and the Byzantine Empire. Because Venice was so different, the expression of both spiritual and material ideals was different in the Venetian Republic. However, Venice was still frequently involved in Crusading well before the Fourth Crusade.

1. MARINO SANUDO'S DESCRIPTION OF VENICE

Marino Sanudo's description of Venice represents one of our few eyewitness accounts of the Most Serene Republic of Venice by one of its more thoughtful historian-citizens. Although his bias is evident, he nonetheless presents a thoughtful portrayal of his hometown. The description of the major buildings and of the manners and customs of the Venetians is especially valuable for its detail, and Sanudo's position as one of the leading citizens of his time gave him special access to particular details not preserved in other sources.

This city of Venice is a free city, a common home to all men, and it has never been subjugated by anyone, as have been all other cities. It was built by Christians, not voluntarily but out of fear [of the army of Attila the Hun], not by deliberate decision but from necessity. Moreover, it was founded not by shepherds as Rome was, but by powerful and rich people, such as have ever been since that time, with their faith in Christ, an obstacle to barbarians and attackers. And, having described its origin, with God's grace I will describe its site and things worthy of record.

This city, amidst the billowing waves of the sea, stands on the crest of the main, almost like a queen restraining its force. It is situated in salt water and built there, because before there were just lagoons, and then, wanting to expand, firm ground was needed for the building of palaces and houses. These are being constructed all the time; they are built above the water by a very ingenious method of driving piles, so that the foundations are in water. Every day the tide rises and falls, but the city remains dry. At times of very low tides, it is difficult to go by boat to wherever one wants. The city is about 7 miles in circumference; it has no surrounding walls, no gates which are locked at night, no sentry keeping watch as other cities have for fear of enemies; it is so very safe at present, that no one can attack or frighten it As another writer has said, its name has achieved such dignity and renown that it is fair to say Venice merits the title "Pillar of Italy," "deservedly it may be called the bosom of all Christendom." For it takes pride of place before all others, if I may say so, in prudence, fortitude, magnificence, benignity and clemency; everyone throughout the world testifies to this. To conclude, this city was built more by divine than human will. But enough of these preliminary matters: let us turn to the main subject.

It is, then, a very big and beautiful city, excelling over all others, with houses and piazze founded upon salt water, and it has a Grand Canal. You can go by galley from a place called Lido (where there are two fortresses at the port of Venice; it is about 2 miles away) to St. Mark's; from there the Grand Canal, which is very wide indeed, takes you as far as Santa Chiara, which is almost where the city begins. And I have seen a galley going up the Canal. On either side there are houses of patricians and others; they are very beautiful, costing from 20,000 ducats downwards; as an example I give the palace belonging to the magnificent Messer Zorzi Comer, most worshipful knight and brother of the Queen of Cyprus; he bought it in our time for 20,000 ducats. Another one of great value is the house which formerly belonged to our late most serene Prince, Francesco Foscari, and now belongs to his heirs. There are many others, which it would take too long to record; I would say there are more than [. . .] worth upwards of 10,000 ducats, and the rest decreasing in value between 10,000 and 3,000 ducats; there are also a few, but very few, of less value, which are being rebuilt. And the houses which overlook the said canal are much sought after, and are valued more highly than the others, particularly those near Rialto or St. Mark's. Property is more valuable in one neighborhood than another if it is near to the Piazza. It must be understood that these houses, or indeed palaces, are built in our particular way, in three or four lofty and beautiful stories, on each of which a household can reside very comfortably, because there are living-rooms, reception rooms and all other amenities. Land is very expensive, and is worth a great deal of money. There is an infinite number of houses valued at upwards of 1300 ducats, with rooms having gilded ceilings, staircases of white marble, balconies and windows all fitted with glass. There are so many glass windows that the glaziers are continually fitting and making them (they are manufactured at Murano as I will tell below); in every district there is a glazier's shop. Many of these houses are rented out to whoever wants them, from one year to a maximum of five years (because by law there can be no leases for a longer period than this) and they are rented out to present-day patricians, some for 100, some for 120 and more ducats a year. These houses, I emphasize, are only for longer terms of residence or occupation; I exclude the others, not available for long tenancy, which are rented out in great number. Almost all the houses, and especially those of a high value (because, as well as on the Grand Canal, there are many beautiful houses in every parish) have a water gate and also a land entrance; for there are innumerable waterways called *rii* which lead out of the Grand Canal and pass through different neighborhoods. Above them are bridges; in olden times these were made of wood, but now they are being rebuilt in stone. There is also a very large wooden bridge over the Grand Canal; it is very high, strong and wide, and crosses the Canal at Rialto, as I shall describe later.

There are two ways of getting about in Venice: by foot, on the dry land, and by boat. Certain boats are made pitch black and beautiful in shape; they are rowed by Saracen negroes or other servants who know how to row them. Mostly they are rowed with one oar, though Venetian patricians and senators and ladies are usually rowed with two oars. In summer the cabins have a high covering to keep off the sun, and a broad one in winter to keep off the rain; the high ones are of satin, and the low sort green or purple wool. These small boats are dismantled at night because they are finely wrought and each one is tied up at its mooring. There is such an infinite number of them that they cannot be counted; no one knows the total. On the Grand Canal and in the rii one sees such a continual movement of boats that in a way it is a marvel. There is easily room on them for four people, comfortably seated within. The basic cost of one of these boats is 15 ducats, but ornaments are always required, either dolphins or other things, so that it is a great expense, costing more than a horse. The servants, if they are not slaves, have to be paid a wage, usually one ducat with expenses, so that, adding it all up, the cost is very high. And there is no gentleman or citizen who does not have one or two or even more boats in the family, according to household, etc.

The population of the city, according to a census which was made, is about 150,000 souls. There are three classes of inhabitants: gentlemen [nobles] who govern the state and republic, whose families will be mentioned below; citizens; and artisans or the lower class. The gentlemen are not distinguished from the citizens by their clothes, because they all dress in much the same way, except for the senatorial office-holders, who during their term of office have to wear the colored robes laid down by law. The others almost always wear long black robes reaching down to the ground, with sleeves open to the elbows, a black cap on the head and a hood of black cloth or velvet. Formerly they wore very large hoods, but these have gone out of fashion. They wear trimmings of four sorts: marten, weasel, fox or even sable—which is worn a lot in winter; also skins and furs of vair and sendal. Soled stockings and clogs are worn in all weathers, silk [under]shirts and hose of black cloth; to conclude, they wear black a lot. And when they are in mourning for a dead relative, they wear shoes and a long gown with a hood over the shoulders, but only for a few days before they change back. They also grow beards for some time: three years for the father, two years for the mother, one year for a brother, etc. The majority are merchants and all go to do business on Rialto, as I shall write below. The women are truly very beautiful; they go about with great pomp, adorned with big jewels and finery. And, when some grand lady comes to see Venice, 130 or more ladies go to meet her, adorned with jewels of enormous value and cost, necklaces worth from 300 up to 1000 ducats, and rings on their fingers set with large diamonds, rubies, sapphires, emeralds and other jewels of great value. There are very few patrician women (and none, shall I say, so wretched and poor) who do not have 500 ducats worth of rings on their fingers, not counting the enormous pearls, which must be seen to be believed. And there are more than 100 of such precious necklaces in the city, as I have said. These ladies of ours during their maidenhood wear veils and long tresses; then they wear a black cape. For the most part they wear silk, and formerly they wore gold cloth, but on account of a decree passed in the Senate they now cannot do so. And, if it were not for the provisions drawn up by the most serene Signoria with regard to their tastes and desires in adornment with jewels and other things, and the regulations enacted, they would be very extravagant. When ladies meet each other (excepting the Doge's wife and daughters, the wives of knights and doctors of learning) precedence is by age, and the same applies to the patricians. They do not uncover their heads except to the Prince, although they exchange polite salutations. At present a much-used form of address to any gentleman in the city is "Magnificence," and all of them are addressed as "Missier." I wanted to write this down because usages vary from city to city and it is sometimes useful to know these things.

Venice is divided into six sestieri [i.e., districts]: three on one side of the Canal, and three on the other. . . . On the near side, their names are Castello, St. Mark's and Canareggio; on the other side are Santa Croce, San Polo and Dorsoduro.

2. THE CHRYSOBULL OF 1082

The **Chrysobull** of 1082, issued by Emperor Alexius I Comnenus in favor of the Venetians, was the most famous and far-reaching of all edicts concerning Byzantine-Western trade relations. According to this **chrysobull**, the Venetians, in return for naval aid to Alexius against the Normans of southern Italy, were released from the payment of any customs duties whatsoever in the course of their trade with Byzantium. Moreover, they were given a special quarter of their own (located on the Golden Horn) in Constantinople, and the right to trade in all the main maritime cities of the empire. It is noteworthy that Byzantine merchants themselves were required to pay the normal customs duties.

No one is ignorant of those things which have been done by the faithful Venetians, how after they had gathered together different types of ships, they came to Epidamnus (which we call Dyrrachium) and how they provided for our assistance numerous seaborne fighting men, how the fleet conquered by force the wicked expedition [of the Normans], and how they lost some of their own men. We also know how even now they continue to be allies, and about those things which have been done by their rowers [*thalattokopi*], men who work on the sea. Even if we should not mention this, everyone knows it perfectly well.

Wherefore, in recompense for their services of this kind, Our Majesty decrees, through this present chrysobull, that the Venetians annually receive a gift of twenty pounds [of gold], so that they might distribute this among their own churches in whatever manner they see fit. We honor the noble doge with the most venerable dignity of *protosebastos* and the full stipend which pertains to it, and we designate this honor not only for the person of [the present] doge, but decree that it be continuous and perpetual for all his successors who will come afterwards and to whom the ducal office is transmitted. We also assign to their patriarch the title of *hypertimos*, that is, "most honorable," with a stipend of twenty pounds. And we give this honor (likewise) not to this one man alone, but to all those who will succeed him, so that the honor might also be continuous and perpetual. We decree also that the most holy church of the Apostle and Evangelist St. Mark in Venice receive every year three *numismata* from every one of all the Amalfitans who own workshops in the great city (Constantinople) and in all of Romania [the empire], since they are under the authority of the same patriarch. In addition, those workshops situated in the quarter of Perama [on the Golden Horn across from Pera], together with their upper chambers, which have an entrance and exit throughout, which extend from the Ebraica (gate) up to the Vigla (gate), both inhabited or uninhabited, and in which Venetians and Greeks stay—all of these we grant to them as factories, as well as three docks (scalae) which end in this aforementioned area. We also grant to St. Akyndinos the property, that is a mill, lying alongside this church, which belongs to the house of Peter and which has an income of twenty bezants (Byzantine gold coins). Similarly, we give the church of the Holy Apostle Andrew in Dyrrachium, together with all the imperial payments, except the one which is set aside there to be given to the (harbor) barges.

It is also granted to the Venetians that they may conduct business in every type of merchandise in all parts of the empire that is around great Laodicea, Antioch, Mamistra, Adana, Tarsus, Attalia, Strobilos, Chios, Ephesus, Phocea, Dyrrachium,Valona, Corfu, Bonditza, Methone, Coron, Nauplia, Corinth, Thebes, Athens, Negropont, Demetrias, Thessalonika, Chrysopolis Perithorion, Abydos, Redestos, Adrianople, Apros, Heraclea, Selymbria, and the megalopolis itself [Constantinople], and indeed in all other places which are under the authority of our pious clemency, without their paying anything at all for any favor of commerce or any condition on behalf of their business—[payments] which are made to the fisc, *such as the xylokalamos, limenatukas, portatikos, kanusktos, hexafolleos archontikios* [i.e., charges for mooring ships, disembarking, etc., and taxes on unloading cargo, and taxes on imports, exports, purchases and sales], and exemption from all other taxes which are to be paid to engage in commerce.

For in all places of business Our Majesty has given them the permission that they be free of such exactions. And the Venetians are removed from the authority of the *eparchos parathalassito* himself, the *heleoparochos*, the *genikos*, the *chartularii*, the *hypologoi*, and of all officials of this sort. Le no one who carries out the imperial or other duties presume to be contemptuous of the provisions which have been specified here.

For permission has been granted to the Venetians to deal in whatever types of goods and merchandise anyone may mention and they have the ability to make any purchase and remain free from all exactions.

3. MARTINO DA CANALE'S *HISTORY OF VENICE* (C. 1270)

Martino da Canale's History of Venice presents another detailed view of the Most Serene Republic, albeit from two generations after the Fourth Crusade. He provides many important details that contextualize Venice's role in the wider Christian world. His attention to structural details—such as the office of the doge, the republic's engagement with the Crusading movement, and the religious heritage of the Venetian Republic—make his account especially valuable for the study of Venice in the thirteenth century.

Canale's Description of Venice and Its Doge

[In this book,] I worked diligently and assiduously, to discover the ancient history of the Venetians: where they had come from originally and then afterwards, how they created the noble city that is called Venice, which is now the most attractive and pleasant of our age, filled with beauty and all good things: merchandise flows through this noble city like water through fountains. Venice rises out of the sea, and salt water runs through it and around every place except in the houses and the streets. And when the citizens are in the public squares, they can return to their houses either by land or by water. Commercial goods come from everywhere, along with merchants who buy the products they desire, which they then take back to their own countries. In this city, one can find an enormous amount of food, bread and wine, fowl and water birds, fresh and salted meats, and great fish from the sea or from the river; there are merchants from everywhere who come to buy and sell. In this beautiful city there are a great number of gentlemen, including the old, the middle-aged, and the young, the nobility of whose birth warrants great praise; with them, merchants who buy and sell, money changers and citizens practicing every craft, mariners of all sorts and boats that transport them to any locale, and warships used to cause injury to the enemy. Also in this city there are many beautiful ladies, maidens, and girls, in abundance, very richly clothed.

I have told you how the great city called Venice was founded and I will now tell you about the succession of doges who governed the Venetians and the victories won by the Venetians in the time of each doge. The first doge of the Venetians was Mesire Paulicio, who held the noble dogeship in the first city that the Venetians built after Attila the pagan had destroyed the cities of Italy. But first I would like you to know about the nobility of the Venetian doges: you should know that Monseignor the doge of Venice wears a crown, and wherever he goes, a sword is carried, which a nobleman bears. And on solemn feast days the noble doge wears a golden crown encrusted with jewels on his head, and wears clothing made of cloth of gold. And wherever he goes on solemn feast days, he is followed by a young lad who carries an ombrellino [i.e., a ceremonial umbrella] made of cloth of gold over his head, and before him, another lad carries a beautiful faldstool [i.e., folding chair] and another lad carries a cushion covered with cloth of gold, and he is always followed by his sword, carried by a nobleman.

I will now tell you about the acts of submission by the surrounding cities; every year, the patriarch of Aquileia gives the doge twelve loaves of bread, not small ones but remarkably large ones as well as twelve large, heavy pigs. . . . And when the doges wish to arm more than thirty ships, every city in Istria contributes its men. Some cities provide enough men from their city for Monseignor the doge to arm a galley, and others provide fewer. One of the doges of Venice gave the wine to the patriarch of Grado, because he was impoverished; this patriarch is the patriarch of Venice, who has his seat in Grado. This city was built by the Venetians after the destruction wrought by Attila. . . . And a doge gave the oil from Istria to the church of Monseignor St. Mark. . . . And every year, each city gives to Monseignor the doge a great quantity of silver coins as tribute, and they call the doge their liege lord. And every year the Paduans give a

tribute of linen from their region to the lady dogaressa, the wife of the doge.

How St. Mark Came to Venice

And it was during the time of the doge Giustiniano that the body of Monseignor St. Mark the Evangelist came to Venice, and I will tell you how. It seems that there was a Venetian ship in Alexandria at this time, and in this city were kept the precious remains of Monseignor St. Mark, who the infidels had killed because he revealed to them the faith of Jesus Christ and of holy baptism. But on the Venetian ship that was in Alexandria, there were two men, the first called Mesire Rustico Torcellano. . . . The second brave man who was with Mesire Rustico was called Mesire Tribuno of Malamocco; there was also a third called Staurazio. These three brave men had so fervently hoped to bring back the remains of Monseignor St. Mark to Venice that in the end they were able to do so. They had gone so often to visit the man who guarded Monseignor St. Mark's body that they became his friends. So they said to him, "Sire, if you would like to come with us to Venice, and bring the remains of Monseignor St. Mark there with us, we will make you a very rich man." And when the good man, whose name was Mesire Theodore, heard this, he said, "Keep quiet, my good men, and do not speak of this again, for there is no way in the world that this will happen; the pagans cherish him more than anything in the world, and if they knew that this was your desire, all the gold in the world could not keep them from cutting off your heads." And then one of them answered and said, "Let us wait until the blessed Evangelist convinces you to come with us." They said nothing more about it at this time. But it so happened that it entered this good man's heart to take Monseignor St. Mark's body from there and go back to Venice with him. So he said to these good men, "Gentlemen, how can we remove the holy remains of Monseignor St. Mark from here so that no one will know about it?" And one of them said that they would do it wisely and well. So they went back as quickly as they could to the vault and took out the body of Monseignor St. Mark from where it was, put it in a basket, covered it with cabbages and pork flesh, took another body and put it in the same vault and in the same clothes that had covered the blessed remains of Monseignor St. Mark, and sealed up the vault just as it had been before. And the two good men took the body of Monseignor St. Mark and carried it to their boat in this same basket that I mentioned to you before. And because they feared the pagans, they placed the remains between two sides of pork and hoisted it up on the mast of the boat. And they did this because the pagans will not touch pork flesh.

What can I say? At the same instant that they opened the alcove, a wonderful and intense fragrance spread throughout the city, so great that if all the spices of the world were in Alexandria, it would not have equaled that marvelous aroma. And the pagans said, "Mark is moving!" because they were accustomed to smelling this fragrance each year. Therefore, they went to the vault and they opened it and saw the body I told you about, that the Venetians had put in and dressed in the garments of Monseignor St. Mark, and they were satisfied. But there were a few pagans who came on the boat and searched it throughout, for they were sure that the Venetians had Monseignor St. Mark's remains on their ship. But when they saw the meat up on the mast, they began to shout, "Hanzir, hanzir!" which means, "Pig, pig!" and they jumped from the ship. The wind was good and formidable, and they straightened the sails in the wind and set off on the high sea. . . .

The ship sailed so quickly each day that the holy body of Monseignor St. Mark soon arrived in Venice: and there it was heartily welcomed, as is demonstrated by the beautiful church, the beautiful square and the devotion that the Venetians have to him. For no sooner had he come to Venice than the people placed their hopes in him and ceded dominion of Venice to him, and carried before them the holy image of the Blessed Evangelist; and this occurred in the year of Our Lord Jesus Christ 800, on the last day of January, and each year on this day the Venetians have a great feast in honor of Monseignor St. Mark. And if anyone would like to verify any of the things I have told you, come and look upon the beautiful church of Monseignor St. Mark in Venice, and look right in front of the beautiful church, for the whole story that I have told you is written upon it. And, as Monseignor the apostle has confirmed, those who visit this beautiful church shall have a grand indulgence of seven years. And after the Venetians had built such a beautiful church, they decided that it should be enriched each year in perpetuity, which they did. And this church belongs to Monseignor the doge.

Venice and the Crusades

In fact, the Christians crossed the seas and captured Acre and Jerusalem, but the Venetians had not yet crossed the sea, but when they did, they captured Jaffa. And when Monseignor the bishop Enrico Contarini, who was lord and captain of the Venetian forces, was in possession of Jaffa he said to the Venetians, "Gentlemen, since God has given us this castle, let us make the most of it. Let all the Venetians come here and let them buy and sell their goods." What can I tell you? The Venetians did exactly as Monseignor the bishop said, because they brought their ships to Jaffa. And when the barons of Acre saw that the Venetians had a port of call at Jaffa, they said that Acre was worth nothing, and they talked among themselves and agreed that if the Venetians had been willing to give them their castle, they would have given them a good part of Acre. And so they went to the Venetians to see if they wanted to do this, and they agreed; the Venetians would have a portion of Acre in exchange for Jaffa, which they would give to the Kingdom [of Jerusalem] and to the barons. . . . In this way, the prestige of Monseignor the doge grew enormously, because he sent a Venetian bailiff to the city, who governs the Venetians there, maintained the city, and along with the other barons, defends the city from the pagans and from any other men who want to do harm to the city. And with this, I will say no more about Monseignor the bishop Enrico Contarini, who, upon his return, went to Patras [in the Byzantine Empire] and took from there the bodies of St. Nicholas the bishop and of his uncle St. Nicholas, and of a third saint, who is called Mesire St. N., and brought them back to Venice. . . .

And I will tell you how Mesire Domenico Michiel, the noble doge of Venice, crossed the sea to come to the aid of the Holy Land, which had been greatly damaged, and I will tell you what type of damage this was. You should know the truth, that Mesire Baldwin, the king of Jerusalem, had been captured and imprisoned by the infidels and a great number of knights had been taken with him. And because of this, the patriarch of Jerusalem and the barons of the Holy Land sent for help from Monseignor [i.e., the pope] and from the barons from the other side of the sea, and they also asked the doge of Venice, named Mesire Domenico Michiel. And he set off, along with other men of Venice, and their deeds are well worth recounting, and I will tell it all to you here, how and what they did when they came to the aid of the Holy Land across the sea. . . . So Monseignor the doge, Mesire Domenico Michiel, had a large and wonderful ship prepared. And shortly thereafter, Monseignor the doge boarded the ship, and along with him came the Venetian nobility, and they put out to sea, left Venice, and moved so far across the sea that they arrived in Syria. And the result was that they took eleven pagan ships and other ships loaded with merchandise, and they took Ascalon. What can I say to you? Monseignor the doge, along with his whole army and in the company of the barons of France, went directly to Tyre and attacked the city, but the pagans defended it so well that the Christians gained nothing, and so they began a siege around it. One day, it so happened that the barons heard that other pagans were going to arrive and help the city of Tyre, and the barons reported it to Monseignor the doge, and he told them, "Do not be afraid, for the city will not be so strongly defended

against us that we cannot take it." "In the name of God," said one of the barons, "sir doge, you have your ship ready, and so you are not afraid to stay here, because if the pagans arrive, you can board immediately and be on your way." And when Monseignor the doge heard that, he ordered that all the Venetians pull their ships immediately onto dry land. . . . It happened one day that a dove flew towards Heathendom and passed over the army encamped around Tyre. As the dove passed over, there came from everywhere a cry so great and so marvelous, that the dove, because of its simple, delicate nature, became much disorientated. Blood seeped from it and its wings failed. And then the dove fell to the earth and was quickly captured, and they discovered that it had a letter, and it was brought to Monseignor the doge and to the barons, and the letter was taken and the seal broken. And there was one among them who knew how to read the Saracen letters, which said, "The Sultan of Babylon greets the lord of Tyre and the knights and soldiers and all the pagans of the city," and he wrote to tell them that they should guard the city for fifteen days because, however distressed they were, he would provide them some relief, and if their resistance was lagging, he would revive them. And if they were low on food, he would give them plenty; and they should be certain that in fifteen days he would arrive in Tyre with such a large number of pagans that if all of Christianity were there, he would still defeat them.

When Monseignor the doge and the French barons had heard the letter, they were very disturbed and said that there was no reason for them to remain there.

"In the name of God," said Monseignor the doge of Venice, "leave it to me, and tomorrow I will deliver the city to you." And quickly he had a letter written in Saracen, which read, "The sultan of Babylon greets the lord of Tyre and the knights and the soldiers, and because they were so disturbed, he was very angry, and if he could improve the situation, he would do so willingly. You sent us a letter saying that you had no food left and that you wanted me to come to your aid; you should know that I can bring no help in the way of foodstuffs as I am taken up with important business. If you cannot defend yourselves, give the city to the Christians and save your lives."

When the letter was written, all in Saracen, a skilled goldsmith who was there made a seal similar to that of the Sultan of Babylon; the letter was sealed and tied to the dove, and they let it loose. When the dove was set free, it took up its route and went on its way to Tyre. And when the pagans of Tyre found the dove and the letter that it carried, they were overwhelmed with happiness. They took the letter and broke the seal, and found inside the writing, just as I told you about. They were very downhearted, and they immediately surrendered Tyre to the Christians. Monseignor the doge received one third of the city and the environs, and the barons had the remaining two parts. They then entered the city and took possession of their own sectors. And Monseignor the doge immediately had the ships repaired that he himself had ordered to be damaged, as I mentioned before, and when the boats were ready, he had them put back in the water. What can I tell you? After fifteen days, the Sultan of Babylon came there with such a great number of pagans, that, if they had found the Christians outside of the city and there had been ten times as many of them, they still would have lost their heads. And when the sultan of Babylon saw that he had lost the city, he was greatly infuriated. And so he retreated immediately with his whole force. And Monseignor the doge of Venice left his bailiff in Tyre and then boarded his ship and returned to Venice.

In this part, history relates how after the death of Monseignor Domenico Morosini, Mesire Vitale Michiel, who was noble and wise and courageous, was the doge of Venice. He was harshly assailed with a long and hard war, and I will tell you about it. You should know that it is true that in the course of one day, the emperor Manuel, the lord of Constantinople, had all the Venetians who were in the Empire of Romania seized—this was in the

year 1171—along with all their ships and their goods. But the news, which travels quickly throughout the world, arrived in Venice. And when Monseignor the doge heard the report, he was greatly vexed, and therefore he wasted no time and quickly ordered that trees be cut down and that carpenters come in from everywhere to construct one hundred completely new galleys in one hundred days. You should know, gentlemen, that truly, the Venetians at this time were men of such valor and vigor that none of them thought anything of constructing one hundred galleys to travel to Romania in so short a time.

What can I tell you? Within these hundred days, the great doge of Venice Mesire Vitale Michiel boarded one ship and the Venetian nobles and the people of Venice boarded the other ships, and they departed from Venice, and powered by the wind and by the force of their oars, they soon arrived in Romania. And when Mesire Vitale Michiel, the great doge of Venice, found himself in Romania, he ordered the Venetians who were with him in the ship to seize the cities and the castles immediately and burn them. What should I say? Then the Venetians sallied forth. [The story cuts off here because of a gap in the manuscript. What happens is that the expedition goes horribly wrong, the Venetian fleet is almost completely destroyed, and Doge Michiel is assassinated by an angry mob when he makes it back to Venice.]

Venice and the Fourth Crusade

In the year 1202 of the incarnation of Our Lord Jesus Christ, the count of Saint-Pol and the count of Flanders, the count of Savoy and the marquis of Montferrat sent their messengers to the noble doge of Venice, Mesire Enrico Dandolo, and requested that he furnish ships for them to travel to the Holy Land. And when Monseignor the doge Enrico Dandolo heard the request that the messengers of the French barons had made on behalf of their lords, he was very happy and said to the messengers, "Speak thus to your lords; that, at whatever moment they would like to come to Venice, they will find the fleet ready to travel to the Holy Land," and that he himself wanted to cross with them in the service of the Holy Church. So the messengers returned to their lords and told them everything just as Monseignor the doge had directed them. And when the barons of France heard this, they were very happy, both about the fleet that Monseignor the doge had promised them and because the doge himself would travel with them to the Holy Land, and they said that they could ask for no better company in the entire world.

Mesire Enrico Dandolo, the noble doge of Venice, ordered carpenters to come and quickly prepare and then construct numerous *chalandres* and carracks and galleys; and he promptly had silver money coined to give to the masters their pay and the rest of what they required, because the lower-value coins that were in use then did not serve their purposes. And it was in the time of Monseignor Enrico Dandolo that they first minted the noble silver coins that are called ducats, which circulate worldwide, because of their value. The Venetians proceeded quickly to ready their ships, and the French, when they were ready, began their journey and rode their horses until they came to Venice, where they were welcomed by the Venetians with great joy and with great celebration. And Monseignor the apostle had sent them his legate, who absolved them of their sins, and Monseignor the doge honored this legate greatly, and took the holy cross from his hands, and many noble Venetians took it as well, along with the commoners.

With great joy and celebration, Mesire Enrico Dandolo boarded a ship to cross the sea with the barons of France in the service of the Holy Church. And each baron boarded his own ship, and the knights boarded the *chalandres* and the other ships where their horses had been placed. And when they had put out to sea, the sailors hoisted the sails into the wind and launched the boats into the sea at full sail, powered by the wind. And Monseignor the doge left his son, who was named Mesire Renieri Dandolo, in his place in Venice; he ruled the Venetians and Venice very wisely.

Section Four
The Greek and Latin Churches in Conflict

The languages of Latin and Greek were two of the most influential in the ancient Mediterranean and two of the most important to the history of Christianity in the medieval world. Problematically, the cultural differences between the western half of the Christian world (which spoke vernacular varieties of Latin) and the eastern half (which spoke varieties of Greek) were numerous and significant enough to cause real friction between the religious organizations that governed church practices in the same regions. By the heart of the Middle Ages, these tensions erupted in a variety of doctrinal, practical, and philosophical contests that threatened to create two diametrically opposed camps: one Latin, one Greek. These conflicts often were expressed in terms of a shared history but rarely stayed on specific topics for long; quarrels over the wordings of important points of doctrine could often be paired with the choice to use leavened or unleavened bread in the Mass. While these may seem petty to modern eyes, the medieval world was one where religious questions were not simply matters of internal faith but had a real (i.e., perceived) impact on the affairs of the world and on the eternal afterlife to which all Christians nominally subscribed. It is crucial to remember that whatever they might disagree on, the power of God (expressed in the exercise of religious ritual) and the importance of the immortal soul were never in doubt between the two sides. Religious leaders were held responsible for their followers' salvation (i.e., if a parishioner was damned, the priest was partially responsible), so the use of excited language and harsh tones reflects the concern that (to borrow a commonly used medieval metaphor) if one part of their spiritual body (a follower or a parish) were to become infected with the wrong practices, it would soon metastasize and infect all parts of the Christian world; such an event would lead everyone to the fiery pits of a hell that was all too real for medieval Christians.

1. POPE NICHOLAS I'S AFFIRMATION OF PAPAL SUPREMACY OVER THE EASTERN CHURCH (865/6)

Because the bishops of Rome (i.e., the popes) were the acknowledged head of the western church, they often acted as a court of final appeals on ecclesiastical matters. Since the time of the Emperor Constantine in the fourth century, the bishops of Rome also claimed to be the highest spiritual authorities on earth, since they derived their power from the founder of their diocese, the Apostle Peter, to whom Jesus gave the authority to build the Christian church. This often led to disputes with the Eastern Church, whereby the papacy asserted this theoretical and legal supremacy to little effect.

If you seek to learn from us, as from ministers of Christ and dispensers of his mysteries, we shall show you quite clearly. But if you truly consider it unimportant to learn and you lift up your steps against the privileges of the Roman church, beware lest they be turned against you. Indeed, it is hard for you to struggle against the slow of a river and hard to kick against the pricks. Then if you do not hear us, let it be so . . . especially since the privileges of the Roman church of Christ, made firm in the mouth of the Blessed Peter, deposited in the church itself, observed from antiquity, and celebrated by the holy ecumenical synods perpetually venerated by all churches, in no way may be diminished, in no way infringed upon, in no way altered, since the basis which God established no human should dare to move, and that which God has established remains firm and valid. . . .

These privileges of this holy church—given by Christ, not by synods, privileges both celebrated and venerated, which have brought us not so much honor as burden, although we have obtained this honor not through our merits but by command of the grace of God through the blessed Peter and in the blessed Peter—oblige and compel us to have solicitude for all the churches of God. For the company of the blessed Apostle Paul was added to that of the Blessed Peter. These, like two great lights of heaven, having been divinely placed in the Roman church, have illuminated magnificently the whole world by the splendor of their brightness. Like the reddening sun, they give luster from themselves as well as through their disciples, as if they were shining rays of light. Through their presence, the West has been made [the equal] of the East. . . . These things, then, I say compel [me] to aid Ignatius, the patriarch, as a brother who has been deposed by no rule or ecclesiastical order. For among other things, he [i.e., Peter] through whom all these privileges are given to us, heard from God: "Whenever you are able . . . help your brother."

These divinely inspired privileges have mandated that—because Photius, with Ignatius still alive, not through the [proper] entry but from another place ascended to the Lord's flocks, overthrew the shepherd, and dispersed our sheep—he must move away from the position which he has usurped and from the communions of Christians. And since we consider nothing about the positions of Ignatius or Photius more discreet, mild, or useful than that each should come to an investigation to be renewed in Rome, we desire this greatly and we admonish you for your own good that you assent.

2. PHOTIUS CHARGES ROME WITH DOCTRINAL DEVIATION (867)

While the bishops of Rome claimed legal and spiritual authority over the patriarch of Constantinople, they did not do so without challenges from the city of Constantine. One of the most common charges that the patriarchs of Constantinople levied against the bishops of Rome was that the Roman Church made grave errors in the interpretations of key religious and legal questions, in particular with respect to the wording of key religious statements of belief. The fulminations of the patriarch of Constantinople, described here, were but one chapter in a long series of mutual reprisals between Rome and Constantinople.

Where have you learned this [i.e., that the Holy Spirit proceeds from the Son]? From what Gospel is this term taken: From which council does this blasphemy come? Our Lord and God says, "the Spirit which proceeds from the Father." But the fathers of this new impiety state, "the Spirit which proceeds from the Son."

Who will not close his ears against the enormity of this blasphemy? It goes against the Gospel, it is arrayed against the Holy Synods, and it contradicts the blessed and holy Fathers: Athanasius the great, Gregory renowned in theology, the [royal] robe of the Church (who is) the great Basil, and the golden-mouth of the ecumene, that sea of wisdom truly named Chrysostom. But why should I mention this Father or that one? This blasphemous term: which militates against is at the same time armed against even the holy prophets, the Apostles, bishops, martyrs, and the voice of God himself. . . .

We are not discussing worldly affairs. The right to judge them rests with the Emperor and with the secular tribunal. But here it is a question of divine and heavenly decisions and those are reserved only to him to whom the Word of God has said: "Whatsoever you shall bind upon earth, will be bound in Heaven and whatsoever you shall loose on earth, shall be loosed in Heaven" (Matt. 16:19). And who are the men to whom this order was given—the Apostles and their successors. And who are their successors—he who occupies the throne of Rome and is the first; the one who sits upon the throne of Constantinople and is the second; after them, those of Alexandria, Antioch and Jerusalem. That is the Pentarchic authority in the Church. It is to them that all decision belongs in divine dogmas. The Emperor and the secular authority have the duty to aid them and to confirm what they have decided.

3. THE PATRIARCH OF CONSTANTINOPLE'S SPOKESMAN CRITICIZES LATIN RELIGIOUS PRACTICES (1054)

Beyond doctrinal questions, the Greek and Latin Churches disagreed on a number of basic practical questions that represented how deeply they differed. By the eleventh century, these were so specific that the two sides even disagreed as to whether the bread used for the Eucharist should be unleavened (that is, without yeast) like the bread eaten at Jewish Passover Seders (like the Last Supper), or if it should be leavened bread to depart from the customs of Judaism and to denote that Jesus "rose" in both body and bread. This was called the *azyma* debate by the Greeks. While these disagreements may seem petty to modern eyes, a mistake on the fundamental question of the sacraments put the immortal souls of the parishioners at risk; the disagreement was no small matter.

God's great love and the depth of his compassion have persuaded me to your sanctity, and through you to all the archbishops of the Franks and to the most venerable pope himself, in order to mention the question of the *azyma* and of the Sabbath, in which [practices] you improperly commune with the Jews in the manner of the Mosaic law. For those [i.e., the Jews] were instructed by Moses to observe the Sabbath and [the practice of] the *azyma*. But Christ is our Paschal (Lamb), who, so as not to be considered pagan, was circumcised and at first celebrated the lawful Passover, and after ceasing [to observe] that, inaugurated a new practice for us. The holy evangelist, in the Gospel according to Matthew concerning the Last Supper, speaks thus: "On the first Friday of the Passover festival, Jesus' disciples came to him saying, "Lord, where do you wish that we prepare for you the Passover festival? . . ."

[Passage follows on Jesus' and the Apostles' Passover.]

But since this [Jewish] law has ceased, the azyma, of necessity, according to the same Apostle, also ceased. [And the same thing has occurred] in connection with the paralytic, whom he [i.e., Jesus] made whole on the Sabbath, and because of this [i.e., Jesus' non-observance of the Jewish Sabbath], the ones who keep the Sabbath and also the *azyma*, saying that they are Christians, are neither good Jews nor good Christians. Rather, they are similar to the skin of a leopard, as Basil the Great tells us, of which the hair was neither black nor wholly white.

These things, O man of God, you, knowing many times over and having taught them thus to your own people, and having written them, now order these things to be changed among those who follow the same practice, so you may gain the salvation of your own soul. Also send to the archbishops and bishops of the [episcopal] thrones of Italy, and have them take an oath that they will change these things in order that you may have the greatest reward both in these two letters as in other good things of yours. And if you do this I will write to you in a second of greater and more extensive matters as further evidence of the true and divine faith and glory of God and the salvation of those choosing to believe correctly in the orthodox manner, for whom Christ gave his own soul.

4. THE BYZANTINE BISHOP OF NICOMEDIA'S MODERATE VIEWS ON PAPAL PRIMACY (1036)

Despite the proclamations of the bishop of Rome or the patriarch of Constantinople, there were a number of prelates who found a kind of middle ground. Respect for the political importance of Rome, while maintaining Greek theological traditions, perhaps evinces the kind of straddling that moderate bishops caught between Rome and Constantinople had. For many, the matters of conscience—like dogma and practice—were made more complicated by the political machinations of contemporary nobles and politically ambitious clergymen. The bishop of Nicomedia, here, presents a moderate view on Rome's claims while still maintaining a fundamentally Greek-oriented allegiance.

I neither deny nor do I reject the Primacy of the Roman Church whose dignity you have extolled.

As a matter of fact, we read in our ancient histories that there were three patriarchal sees closely linked in brotherhood, Rome, Alexandria, and Antioch, among which Rome, the highest see in the empire, received the primacy. For this reason Rome has been called the first see and it is to her that appeal must be made in doubtful ecclesiastical case, and it is to her judgment that all matters that cannot be settled according to the normal rules must be submitted.

But the Bishop of Rome himself ought not to be called the Prince of the Priesthood, nor the Supreme Priest, nor anything of that kind, but only the Bishop of the first see. Thus it was that Boniface III (607), who was Roman by nationality, and the son of John, the Bishop of Rome, obtained from the Emperor Phocas confirmation of the fact that the apostolic see of Blessed Peter was the head of all the other Churches, since at that time, the Church of Constantinople was saying it was the first see because of the transfer of the Empire in order to make sure that all the sees' gates to each of them telling them that they should be diligent in the preservation. When Constantinople was granted the second place in the hierarchy because of the transfer of the capital, this custom of the delegations was likewise extended to that see.

We find that, my dear brother, written in the ancient historical documents. But the Roman Church to which we do not deny the primacy among her sisters, and whom we recognize as holding the highest place in any general council, the first place of honor, that Church has separated herself by her pretensions. She has appropriated to herself the monarch which is not contained in her office and which has divided the bishops and the churches of the East and West since the partition of the Empire. When, as a result of these circumstances, she gathers a council of the Western bishops without making us (in the East) a part of it, it is fitting that her bishops should accept its decrees and observe them with the veneration that is due to them. . . . But although we are not in disagreement with the Roman Church in the matter of the Catholic faith, how can we be expected to accept these decisions which were taken without our advice and of which we know nothing, since we were not at that same time gathered in council? If the Roman Pontiff, seated upon his sublime throne of glory, wishes to fulminate against us and to launch his orders from the height of his sublime dignity, if he wishes to sit in judgment on our Churches with a total disregard of our advice and solely according to his own will, as he seems to wish, what brotherhood and what fatherhood can we see in such a course of action? Who could ever accept such a situation? In such circumstances we could not be called nor would we really be any longer sons of the Church but truly its slaves.

5. ODO OF DEUIL'S VIEW OF THE GREEK CHURCH IN THE MID-TWELFTH CENTURY

Odo of Deuil was a Frankish monk who accompanied King Louis VII of France on the Second Crusade. As an eyewitness to many of the conflicts that beset that campaign, his view was typical of many at his time: the Byzantine Empire had hamstrung the efforts of the Crusaders from the moment they entered Byzantine territory. His view of Byzantine religious practices made clear that the differences between Latin and Greek Churches were startling to contemporaries unfamiliar with them.

If our priests celebrated mass on Greek altars, the Greeks afterwards purified them with propitiatory offerings and ablutions, as if they had been defiled. All the wealthy people have their own chapels, so adorned with paintings, marble, and lamps that each magnate might justly say, "O lord, have cherished the beauty of Thy house." . . . But, O dreadful thing! We heard of an ill usage of theirs which could be expiated by death; namely, that every time they celebrate the marriage of one of our men, if he has been baptized the Roman way, they re-baptize him before they make the pact. We know heresies of theirs, both concerning their

treatment of the Eucharist and concerning the procession of the Holy Ghost. . . . Actually, it was for these read the Greeks had incurred the hatred of our men, for their error had become known even among the lay people. Because of this they were judged we Christians, and the Franks considered killing them a matter of no importance and hence could with the more difficulty be restrained from pillage and plundering. . . . Since the Greeks celebrate this feast [of St. Dionysius], the emperor sent over to the king a carefully selected group of his clergy, whom he had equipped with a large taper decorated elaborately with a variety of colors; and thus he increased the glory of the ceremony. Those clergy certainly differed from ours as to words and order of service, but they made a favorable impression because of their sweet chanting; for the mingling of the voices, the heavier with the light, the eunuch's, namely, with the manly voice (for many of them were eunuchs), softened the hearts of the Franks. And they gave the onlookers pleasure by their graceful bearing and gentle clapping of hands and genuflections.

6. GREEK CITIZENS UNDER LATIN RULE PROPOSE A DUAL PATRIARCHATE (C. 1210)

Cities normally had only one bishop in charge of the religious activities in the city, but in some rare instances, the necessity for parallel power structures became overwhelming. In particular, the solution prevalent in the Holy Land was that each Christian sect maintained separate religious leaders who shared access to holy sites and respected their fellow leaders' authority over their own communities. These hybrid structures of power were highly unusual then, but not without precedent. The following is a petition by Greek subjects to their Latin lord to institute such a dual patriarchate.

Many patriarchs and emperors have desired to see that day [of the union of the two churches], but this they were denied. You, Lord, after the passing of many generations, shall be granted this grace, to unite East and West, and you shall become and be called the thirteenth Apostle. . . . Since, then, small is the gap between Latins and Greeks which loosens the unity of the one church, seek to assemble an ecumenical council and send out representatives of your Magnificence, and let it be proclaimed, and let all that is in doubt be resolved. If you yourself be the coworker of God, according to Paul the great Apostle, we are ready, Lord, even to leave the jurisdictional authority . . . and to attend a council to be held in East or West. . . . For this reason we write daily to our Western brothers of this area, both cocelebrants and cobishops, to be ready to assemble. . . .

But it is necessary before that council that we have a patriarch of our own views and of our language who may teach and hand down our customs and receive our confession. For that reason, both in Jerusalem and in Antioch where there is one king, there are two prelates, one for the Greek and one for the Latin of the same teachings and language and thus similar to each [people]. For it is not proper to confess your secret through an interpreter to a patriarch of another language, even if perhaps agreement of opinion exists. Thus these considerations should be observed until union is accomplished.

7. THE GREEK PATRIARCH ANTHONY DEFENDS THE ROLE OF THE EMPEROR IN THE CHURCH (1395)

One of the most notable differences in the way the Greek Church operated on a daily basis was the role played by the emperor. While in the Latin world the emperor was forbidden from appointing bishops and deciding on religious questions, in the Byzantine Empire the emperor followed in the traditions of Constantine and took a more direct and hands-on approach to the governing of the Church. Here, the Greek patriarch lays out the reasons why the emperor's influence was, contrary to Roman suspicions, a beneficial relationship for the Byzantines. By offering a defense of caesaropapism, the patri-arch effectively issues his own rebuttal of the larger two swords doctrine. This selection comes from a letter to the Grand Prince of Moscow in the late fourteenth century, but reflects sentiments prevalent for centuries previous to its composition.

The holy emperor has a great place in the church, for he is not like other rulers or governors of other regions. This is so because from the beginning the emperors established and confirmed the [true] faith in all the inhabited world. They convoked the ecumenical councils and confirmed and decreed the acceptance of the pronouncements of the divine and holy canons regarding the correct doctrines and the government of Christians. They struggled boldly against heresies, and imperial decrees together with councils established the metropolitan sees of the archpriests and the divisions of their provinces and the delineation of their districts. For this reason the emperors enjoy great honor and position in the Church, for even if, by God's permission, the nations [primarily the Ottoman Turks] have constricted the authority and domain of the emperor, still to this day the emperor possesses the same charge from the church and the same rank and the same prayers [from the church]. The basileus [i.e., emperor] is anointed with the great myrrh and is appointed basileus and autokrator of the Romans, and indeed of all Christians. Everywhere the name of the emperor is commemorated by all patriarchs and metropolitans and bishops wherever men are called Christians, [a thing] which no other ruler or governor ever received. Indeed he enjoys such great authority over all that even the Latins themselves, who are not in communion with our church, render him the same honor and submission which they did in the old days when they were united with us. So much more do Orthodox Christians owe such recognition to him. . . . Therefore, my son, you are wrong to affirm that we have the church without an emperor for it is impossible for Christians to have a church and no empire. The [empire] and the church have a great unity and community—indeed they cannot be separated. Christians can repudiate only emperors who are heretics who attack the church, or who introduce doctrines irreconcilable with the teachings of the Apostles and the Fathers. But our very great and holy [emperor], by the grace of God, is most orthodox and faithful, a champion of the church, its defender and avenger, so that it is impossible for bishops not to mention his name in the liturgy. Of whom, then, do the Fathers, councils, and canons speak? Always and everywhere they speak loudly of the one rightful [emperor], whose laws, decrees, and charters are in force throughout the world and who alone, only he, is mentioned in all places by Christians in the liturgy.

8. AN ACCOUNT OF THE ATTACKS OF EMPEROR ANDRONICUS ON THE LATINS OF CONSTANTINOPLE IN THE 1180S

Although it is not a religious text, the following account of the massacre of Latin Christians in Constantinople under the Emperor Andronicus demonstrates how a religious disagreement had blossomed into a seething antipathy on both sides, so much so that an unpopular usurper would use an anti-Latin massacre as a political tool to win over support from the people. In this contemporary account of the reign of Androni-cus, written by William of Tyre, an archbishop in the crusader-states, consider carefully how these reports widened cultural gulfs between Greeks and Latins and also underlined, for contemporaries, the need for the spiritual sword to receive cooperation.

This change of affairs spread consternation among the Latins, for they feared that the citizens would make a sudden attack upon them; in fact they had already received warning of such intention from certain people who had private knowledge of the conspiracy. Those who were able to do so, therefore, fled from the wiles of the Greeks and the death which threatened them. Some embarked on forty-four galleys which chanced to be in the

harbor, and others placed all their effects on some of the many other ships there.

The aged and infirm, however, with those who were unable to flee, were left in their homes, and on them fell the wicked rage which the others had escaped. For Andronicus, who had secretly caused ships to be prepared, led his entire force into the city. As soon as they entered the gates these troops, aided by the citizens, pushed to that quarter of the city occupied by the Latins and put to the sword the little remnant who had been either unwilling or unable to flee with the others. Although but few of these were able to fight, yet they resisted for a long time and made the enemy's victory a bloody one.

Regardless of treaties and the many services which our people had rendered to the empire, the Greeks seized all those who appeared capable of resistance, set fire to their houses, and speedily reduced the entire quarter to ashes. Women and children, the aged and the sick, all alike perished in the flames. To vent rage upon secular buildings alone, however, was far from satisfying their wickedness; they also set fire to churches and venerated places of every station and burned, together with the sacred edifices, those who had fled for refuge. No distinction was made between clergy and laymen, except that greater fury was displayed toward those who wore the honorable habits of high office or religion. Monks and priests were the especial victims of them and were put to death under excruciating torture.

Among these latter was a venerable man named John, a subdeacon of the Roman church, whom the pope had sent to Constantinople on business related to the church. They seized him and, cutting off his head, fastened it to a filthy dog as an insult to the church. In the midst of such frightful worse sacrilege than parricide, not even the dead, whom impiety itself generally spares, were suffered to rest undisturbed. Corpses were torn from the tombs and dragged through the streets and squares as if the insensate bodies were capable of feeling the indignities offered them.

The vandals then repaired to the hospital of St. John, as it is called, where they put to the sword all the sick they found. Those whose pious duty it should have been to relieve the oppressed, namely the monks and priests, called in footpads and brigands to carry on the slaughter under promise of reward. Accompanied by these miscreants, they sought out the most secluded retreats and the inmost apartments of homes, that none who were hiding there might escape death. When such were discovered, they were dragged out with violence and handed over to the executioners, who, that they might not work without pay, were given the price of blood for the murder of these wretched victims.

Even those who seemed to show more consideration sold into perpetual slavery among the Turks and other infidels the fugitives who had resorted to them and to whom they had given hope of safety. It is said that more than four thousand Latins of various age, sex, and condition were delivered thus to barbarous nations for a price.

In such fashion did the perfidious Greek nation, a brood of vipers, like a serpent in the bosom or a mouse in the wardrobe evilly requite their guests—those who had not deserved such treatment and were far from anticipating anything of the kind; those to whom they had given their daughters, nieces, and sisters as wives and who, by long living together, had become their friends.

9. ROBERT OF CLARI'S DESCRIPTION OF CONSTANTINOPLE (1204)

Robert of Clari was a common soldier who fought on the Fourth Crusade. His history includes one of the best descriptions of the spiritual and temporal wealth of Constantinople in 1204. In this text he describes his travels around the city, especially noting the beauty of the two imperial palaces and the immense trove of relics kept in the personal chapel of the emperor of Constantinople, along with the beauty of the city's main church of Saint Sophia, known in Greek as the Hagia Sophia. There were many reasons why caesaropapism was an effective doctrine for the Greek Church, but the preservation of Constantinople despite attempted conquests and the many ways in which it was one of the most advanced cities in the world likely suggested that God favored Constantinople and the societal and religious order followed by the Constantinopolitans.

When the city was taken and the pilgrims had lodged themselves, even as I have told you, and when the palaces were taken, then were there found in these palaces riches without number. And how rich was the Palace of the Lion's Mouth, and how built, I will tell you now. There were, forsooth, within this palace (which the marquis now held) five hundred chambers, which were all joined one to another; and they were all wrought in mosaic work of gold. Moreover, there were full thirty chapels there, both large and small; and there was one of these which was called the Holy Chapel, that was so rich and so noble that it contained neither hinge nor socket, nor any other appurtenance such as is wont to be wrought of iron, that was not all of silver; nor was there a pillar there that was not of jasper or porphyry or such like rich and precious stone. And the pavement of the chapel was of white marble, so smooth and so clear that it seemed that it was of crystal. And this chapel was so rich that one could not describe to you the great beauty and the great magnificence thereof. Within this chapel were found many precious relics; for therein were found two pieces of the True Cross, as thick as a man's leg and a fathom in length. And there was found the lance wherewith Our Lord had His side pierced, and the two nails that were driven through the midst of His hands and through the midst of His feet. And there was also found, in a crystal phial, a great part of His blood. And there was found the tunic that he wore, which was stripped from Him when He had been led to the Mount of Calvary. And there, too, was found the blessed crown wherewith He was crowned, which was wrought of sea rushes, sharp as dagger blades.

There also was found the raiment of Our Lady, and the head of my Lord Saint John Baptist, and so many other precious relics that I could never describe them to you or tell you the truth concerning them.

And there were some twenty of these chapels, and there were some two hundred chambers, or three hundred, which all adjoined one to another, and they were all wrought in mosaic of gold. And this palace was so rich and so magnificent that one could not describe or relate to you the magnificence and richness thereof.

And in the palace of Blachernae also was very great treasure found, and very rich. For here were found the rich crowns that belonged to the emperors who dwelt there aforetime, and their rich jewels of gold, and their rich raiment of silken cloth, and their rich imperial robes, and rich and precious stones, and other riches so great that one could not number the great treasure of gold and of silver that was found in the palaces and in many places elsewhere in the city.

Then did the pilgrims gaze upon the greatness of the city, and the palaces, and the rich abbeys, and the rich churches, and the great wonders that were in the city; and they marveled very greatly thereat, and much did they marvel at the Church of Saint Sophia and at the riches that were there.

Now will I tell you of the Church of Saint Sophia, how it was built (Saint Sophia, in Greek, signifieth Holy Trinity in our own tongue). The Church of Saint Sophia was altogether round. And there were on the inside of the church, all round about, arches which were borne up by great pillars—very rich pillars, for there was not a pillar that was not either of jasper, or of porphyry, or of other rich and precious stones, nor was there one of these pillars that had not some virtue of healing. For one there was that healed a man of the disease of the reins when he rubbed himself against it, and one that healed folk of the disease of the side, and some that healed them of other diseases. Nor was there any door of this church, or hinge, or socket, or other furnishing such as is wont to be made of iron, that

was not all of silver. And the high altar of this church was so rich that the price thereof could not be reckoned; for the table which lay upon the altar was of gold, and of precious stones all squared and ground, and all fast joined together; which a certain rich emperor caused to be made. And this table was full fourteen feet in length; and about the altar were pillars of silver, which upheld a canopy above the altar, made like to a bell-tower, and all of massive silver. And so rich was it that one could not reckon the price that it was worth.

And the place where the Gospel was read was so rich and so magnificent that we could not describe to you how it was made. Then, adown the church hung full and hundred lustres, nor was there a lustre that hung not by a great chain of silver, as thick as a man's arm; and in each lustre were some five and twenty lamps, or more; nor was there a lustre that was not worth full two hundred silver marks.

By the socket of the great door of the church, which was all of silver, there hung a tube—of what alloy wrought, no man knows—and it was of the size of one of those pipes such as shepherds pipe upon. That tube had this virtue, of which I will tell you. When a sick man who had some disease within his body—as some swelling whereof his belly was swollen within—when such an one put the tube to his mouth, then this tube would lay hold on him, and would suck out all that disease from him, and would make the poison thereof to run out through his throat. And it kept such fast hold on him that it made his eyes to roll and to turn in his head; nor could he release himself there from or ever the tube had sucked all that disease clean out of him. Nevertheless, albeit he that was sickest was longest held by the tube, when a man who was not sick at all put it to his mouth, it held him in no wise whatsoever.

Furthermore, in another part of the city was another church, which was called the Church of the Seven Apostles. And it was said that this church was yet richer and more magnificent than the Church of Saint Sophia; and so great riches and such magnificence were therein that one could in no wise describe the half of the richness and magnificence of this church. And there lay within this church the bodies of seven apostles; and therein also stood the pillar whereto Our Lord was bound or ever He was put upon the cross. And it was said that there also lay the Emperor Constantine, and Helena, and other emperors a many.

Now in another part of the city was yet another wonder, for there was an open space, hard by the Palace of the Lion's Mouth, which was called the Hippodrome of the Emperor's Games. This space was full a crossbow-shot and a half in length, and about one in breadth. Round about this open space were thirty or forty tiers of stairs, where the Greeks went up for to see the games; and there were lodges there, very magnificent and very noble, where sat the emperor and the empress whilst the games were playing, together with other nobles and ladies. And if two games were playing together, then would the emperor and the empress make a wager together that the one of these games would be better played than the other; so, likewise, did all they that were watching the games.

Lengthwise of this space ran a wall, full fifteen feet high and ten feet wide; and on the top of this wall were images of men and of women, of horses, and oxen, and camels, and bears, and lions, and all manner of other beasts, cast in copper, which were so cunningly wrought and so naturally shaped that there is not, in Heathendom or in Christendom, a master so skilled that he could portray or shape images so skillfully as these images were shaped. And these images were wont erstwhile to play, by enchantment; but afterward they played no more at all. And on these Games of the Emperor did the Franks gaze with wonder when they beheld them.

Yet again, in yet another part of the city, was to be seen yet a greater marvel. For there were two pillars; each one of them was, in thickness, thrice the spread of a man's arms, and each was full fifty fathoms high. And on the top of each one of these pillars dwelt a hermit, in little huts which were

there. And there was a passage on the inside of the pillar, whereby one went up thither. And on the outside of these pillars were portrayed and written in prophecy all the happenings that have come to pass in Constantinople or are yet to come. Nor could any happening be known ere yet it had happened; but when it had happened, then went the people thither and mused there, and then did they perceive for the first time and divine the happening. Yea, even the conquest which the Franks made was written and portrayed there, and the ships with which the assault was made whereby the city was taken; nor yet were the Greeks able to see it until it had already come to pass. But after it was come to pass, then went they thither for to muse and to gaze on these pillars; and it was found that the letters which were written on the ships portrayed there declared that from out of the West would come a tall people, shaven with knives of iron, who would conquer Constantinople.

And all these marvels which I have related to you, and still many more which we cannot relate to you, did the Franks find in Constantinople when they had conquered it. Nor do I believe, of my own knowledge, that any man, be he never so skilled in accounting, could number all the abbeys of the city, so many were there of them, both of monks and of nuns, to say nothing of the other churches in the city. And they counted, in round numbers, some thirty thousand priests in the city, both monks and others.

Of the other Greeks—the high, the lowly, the poor, the rich; of the greatness of the city, of the palaces, and of the other wonders which are therein—will we forbear to tell you further; for no earthly man, though he abode never so long in that city, could number or relate all this to you. And if he were to describe to you the hundredth part of the riches and the beauty and the magnificence which were to be found in the abbeys and in the churches and in the palaces and in the city itself, it would seem that he was a liar, nor would ye believe him at all.

Part Six

Suggestions for Further Reading and Glossary

Suggestions for Further Reading

This is just a pared-down list of titles that will help you get started. As with all "Reacting" projects, the more sources—primary and secondary—that you find, the more arrows you will have for your intellectual quiver. A key advantage might be lying in wait for you *or for your adversaries*, so research will be crucial. There are many excellent books for your research, but beware of popular websites not affiliated with universities. The Crusades, and holy wars in general, are a magnet for all manner of conspiracy theorists, alt-right extremists, and ethno-nationalists.

By far the three most important primary sources for the Fourth Crusade are the histories of Geoffrey of Villehardouin, Robert of Clari, and Nicetas Choniates, all of whom were eyewitnesses to the events. The full text of Villehardouin and Clari are available online, however, these are from translations that are around a century old. The most modern translations are listed below. For Clari the best and most modern translation by Peter Noble is very hard to find, so I have also included the much older, but much more widely available, Edgar Holmes McNeal translation listed below. As for Choniates, his description of the historical sack of Constantinople is available online. But as of the date of this book's publication, there is only one published English translation which is likewise listed below.

PRIMARY SOURCES

Allen, S. J., and Emille Emt. *The Crusades: A Reader.* Toronto: University of Toronto Press, 2003.

Andrea, Alfred, ed. *Contemporary Sources for the Fourth Crusade.* Rev. ed. Leiden: Brill, 2008.

Bird, Jessalyn, Edward Peters, and James Powell, eds. *Crusade and Christendom: Annotated Documents in Translation from Innocent III to the Fall of Acre, 1187–1291.* Philadelphia: University of Pennsylvania Press, 2013.

Choniates, Nicetas. *O City of Byzantium: Annals of Niketas Choniates.* Translated by Harry J. Magoulias, Detroit: Fort Wayne University Press, 1984.

Clari, Robert of. *La conquête de Constantinople.* Translated by Peter Noble. Edinburgh: Société Rencevals British Branch, 2005.

Clari, Robert of. *The Conquest of Constantinople.* Translated by Edgar Holmes McNeil. New York: Columbia University Press, 2005.

Geanakoplos, Deno John, ed. *Byzantium: Church, Society, and Civilization Seen through Contemporary Eyes.* Chicago: University of Chicago Press, 1984.

Smith, Caroline, ed. *Joinville and Villehardouin - Chronicles of the Crusades.* New York: Penguin, 2009.

SECONDARY SOURCES

Angold, Michael. *The Fourth Crusade: Event and Context.* New York: Pearson, 2003.

Harris, Jonathan. *Byzantium and the Crusades, Second Edition.* London: Bloomsbury, 2014.

Madden, Thomas F. *Enrico Dandolo and the Rise of Venice.* Baltimore: John Hopkins University Press, 2008.

Madden, Thomas. *The Concise History of the Crusades, Third Student Edition.* Lanham, MD: Rowman & Littlefield, 2013.

Phillips, Jonathan. *The Fourth Crusade and the Sack of Constantinople.* New York: Penguin, 2004.

Queller, Donald, and Thomas Madden. *The Fourth Crusade: The Conquest of Constantinople.* 2nd ed. Philadelphia: University of Pennsylvania Press, 1999.

Riley-Smith, Jonathan. *What Were the Crusades?* 4th ed. San Francisco: Ignatius Press, 2009.

Treadgold, Warren. *A Concise History of Byzantium.* Palgrave, 2001.

Glossary

Abbot. The spiritual and administrative head of a monastery, usually elected for his seniority and the quality of his counsel. Some of the most powerful abbots, like the Cistercian abbot Bernard of Clairvaux, wielded levels of authority that were comparable to the pope, despite being legally subordinate.

Apostolic See. Another name for Rome and, in turn, for the office of the papacy. Medieval popes argued that since Jesus left the administration of his earthly ministry to Peter (Mt 16:18), and since Peter founded the Church in Rome at the end of his earthly life, Rome's church was the most important. While many Christian communities in the late ancient Mediterranean could trace their founding to an apostle, the term "Apostolic See" became, over time, almost exclusively associated with Rome.

Bishop. The spiritual and administrative head of a diocese, usually elected by the cathedral chapter (a group of priests and deacons serving at the cathedral) from their own diocese. Although they were officially appointed by the pope, many bishops were careful to cultivate local networks of patrons and political supporters. Metropolitan bishops were in charge of other bishops, called suffragans. Archbishops held charge over more ancient or prestigious dioceses. Metropolitans were almost always archbishops, but not all archbishops were metropolitans. Most bishops were allowed to keep a crozier (a large staff with a cross on top) for a walking staff and a mitre (a kind of high, pointed hat) to show their positions of office. Occasionally, powerful metropolitans were given a pallium—a kind of cloth, neck-ring sash—that showed they were specially chosen by the pope.

Bull. A special letter from the pope, sealed with a lead, two-sided seal attached to red and yellow threads. These letters pronounced on matters of canon law, theology, or on major political complications of the day. Written in Latin and often highly formulaic, these letters preserved remarkable amounts of detail in their narrative sections.

Charter. A document memorializing a gift or contract between two or more parties. Ranging from a few lines of mediocre Latin on a parchment scrap to the highly ornate Byzantine chrysobull—written in vermillion ink and sealed with a solid gold seal—these documents represent some of the most local and careful primary sources preserved from the medieval world.

Crusade. Usually defined as an armed pilgrimage to Christian holy sites, by the middle of the twelfth century a Crusade was a kind of holy war against the enemies of Christendom called and directed by the pope. Although war was considered sinful in most circumstances, most Crusaders swore a vow to complete their pilgrimage (*peregrinatio*) in exchange for a commutation of their penance. Effectively, completing a Crusade vow wiped all the penalties of previous sins away, provided the penitents had expressed contrition for their misbehaviors.

Diocese. The territory controlled by a bishop. Several dioceses, when controlled by a single metropolitan, comprised an ecclesiastical province.

Doge. The leader of the Most Serene Republic of Venice, elected for life by the adult male citizens of Venice in a series of direct and indirect elections which evolved over time.

Feudalism. This catchall term has fallen out of favor with scholars, but it generally represents a kind of social organization in which lords provide vassals with land, while vassals provide lords with military service. These social bonds created a close connection between lords and vassals, especially when enhanced with ritual and repeated exchanges of gifts.

Fief. The name for the parcel of land that lords gave vassals in exchange for their military support.

Frank. A catchall name, often deployed by Byzantine and Near Eastern authors, to describe peoples living in the former territories of the Carolingian Empire.

Indulgence. The primary spiritual benefit of a Crusade, an indulgence commuted all of the penance assigned for any and all sins that a Crusader confessed before reaching his destination. The indulgence was a particular benefit of the Crusade and was one of the more important inducements for Christians to join the Crusade, since completion of the Crusading vow—nominally, by reaching the destination—commuted all of the penance enjoined on the Crusader.

Investiture. The act of endowing an individual with either a lay or clerical office, usually with a refined ritual and represented by symbols of office—like a ring, staff, sword, or belt. In the case of bishops and abbots, this was usually performed by an ecclesiastical superior; for nobles, it was done by a figure of greater prestige. In the late eleventh and early twelfth centuries, the papacy and the Holy Roman Empire engaged in a major debate about whether the emperor could provide bishops with their investiture, in large part because providing these symbolic gifts was also a recognition of a power disparity.

Just War. Differentiated from Crusades because they did not provide an indulgence for penances, just wars were considered licit and excusable, provided the targets of the war had satisfied the appropriate criteria.

Marshal. An official appointed in the retinues of most medieval noblemen, the marshal was a kind of military leader and organizer, usually the most prominent warrior or strategist among the lord's supporters.

Military Order. A group of knights with a semi-monastic manner of living who were closely associated with the Crusades and the protection of the Holy Land. Examples include the Knights Templar and the Knights Hospitaller.

Monastery. A Christian community designed for spiritual edification and prayer, where penitents focused on their religious growth to ensure they were more likely to find a place in heaven. Because the monks (members of a monastery) were so focused on prayer and religious enlightenment, monasteries often accumulated enormous wealth as the nobility sought to ensure that monks would pray for them after death.

Papacy. The office of the head of the Roman (Latin rite) Church, represented by the bishop of Rome (called a pope). Popes often used legates—officials delegated with papal authority to solve problems—and cardinals to enforce their political and legal agenda in far-flung locales. Because Rome claimed that the diocese of Rome was founded by the Apostle Peter, medieval popes claimed to be the head of all true Christians.

Patriarch. A diocese founded by an apostle was ruled by a patriarch, a kind of higher-tier archbishop. By the early thirteenth century, those of Constantinople (usually called the ecumenical patriarch) and Rome (called the pope) were the most powerful.

Penance. The spiritual practices enjoined on Christians to expiate their sins after they confessed them. Often requiring specific prayer rituals, acts of charity, or a pilgrimage, penance was a major part of the religious calculus of medieval Christianity.

Pilgrimage. A long religious journey, usually to a place of particular holiness. In Christianity, the major pilgrimage centers in the thirteenth century were Canterbury, Santiago de Compostela, Rome, and Jerusalem. When undertaken as penance, the completion of a pilgrimage often came with an indulgence.

Pronoia. The Byzantine equivalent of feudalism, but with limited rights of inheritance from one holder of a territory to another. The revenues and administrative rights, rather than the lands themselves, were the items granted by the emperor or his delegated subordinates and usually required maintenance of imperial armies.

Sacrament. A religious ceremony or ritual that imparts some fashion of divine grace. Examples of major sacraments included baptism, penance, and the Eucharist (the ceremonial recreation of the Last Supper), and these were all under the careful supervision of the priests and bishops in Latin Rite Christianity.

Sebastocrator. The title of sebastocrator was one of the highest titles that could be granted by the Byzantine emperor. The bearer could wear a crown and often was considered second only to the emperor in authority. It was most often given to senior members of the imperial family and close associates.

Tithe. A tenth of all annual income provided to the church. Traditionally, one-sixth of this income was provided to the poor. Payable in cash and in kind (that is, with produce), tithes were often used to fund a variety of projects favored by the church.

Troubadours. Composers of songs and poetry at noble courts, troubadours provided nobles with increased fame and prestige for their deeds. Because they relied on the patronage of the nobles about whom they sang, many troubadours cultivated active and reciprocal relationships with the nobles of several courts.

Usury. The illegal charging of interest to Christians on loans. Because Crusaders' loans were kept in deferment and their lands were under papal protection, charging interest to a Crusader, even at a miniscule rate, was considered usury.

CPSIA information can be obtained
at www.ICGtesting.com
Printed in the USA
LVHW050303140123
737123LV00002B/260